Alexander Moody Stuart

Our Old Bible

Moses on the Plains of Moab. Fourth Edition

Alexander Moody Stuart

Our Old Bible

Moses on the Plains of Moab. Fourth Edition

ISBN/EAN: 9783337100087

Printed in Europe, USA, Canada, Australia, Japan

Cover: Foto ©Lupo / pixelio.de

More available books at **www.hansebooks.com**

MOSES ON THE PLAINS OF MOAB.

BY

A. MOODY STUART, D.D.

FOURTH EDITION.

Edinburgh:
JOHN MACLAREN & SON, PRINCES STREET.
LONDON: JAMES NISBET & CO.
GLASGOW: DAVID BRYCE & SON.

1881.

EDINBURGH
PRINTED BY LORIMER AND GILLIES,
31 ST. ANDREW SQUARE.

CONTENTS.

CHAP.		PAGE
I.	Israel's Witness to Moses and to God on the Plains of Moab,	10
II.	The Book found in the Temple: the Form of Deuteronomy not Dramatic,	14
III.	This Other Side of Jordan,	18
IV.	Theory of a New Code in the Heart of an Old Book,	25
V.	Israel's Service of Song,	32
VI.	The Judicial Cleansing of the Land,	40
VII.	The One Altar,	46
VIII.	The Law of the Firstlings,	53
IX.	The Testimony of Joshua,	59
X.	The Seal of the New Testament,	67

MOSES ON THE PLAINS OF MOAB.

"THIS only book," said an old writer on Deuteronomy, "was that silver brook, out of which the Lord Christ, our champion, chose all those three smooth stones wherewith He prostrated the Goliath of hell in that sharp encounter in the wilderness."

A Biblical critic, by whom the book is denied to Moses, acknowledges that the Deuteronomic lesson, "Man doth not live by bread only, but by every word that proceedeth out of the mouth of the Lord," is a Divine truth, whoever uttered it; and he holds it to be of equal value whether found in the Bible or elsewhere. But the sharpness of the sword with which our Lord thrust back the assault of the Tempter, was not found in the mere rightness of the words, but in the answer that so "it is written;" and the teaching of the Scriptures on their own character is not that there is truth in the Word of God, but that "His Word is truth." In this relation the most remarkable of the three answers taken from Deuteronomy by Christ, is that against the last temptation to gain the dominion of the world by falling down and worshipping its god; we should have expected so blasphemous a proposal to apostasy to be resented and repulsed as openly contrary to all allegiance to the Supreme, and requiring no Scriptural authority to refute it; but Christ so guides Himself by the Word of God, and prizes it so highly, that even in so clear a case He answers, "It is written."

That a book devoutly used and so greatly honoured by our Lord Himself, is now held by men of note amongst us not to be in the words of Moses, in whose name it is given, is the darkest cloud that has brooded over the land in our day, and urgently calls for every light which can be held out to guide the minds of many who are bewildered in its mist.

The present critical theory that Deuteronomy was written by an unknown Jewish prophet for the purpose of bringing the ordinances of Israel down to the times of the later kings of Judah, is so broadly contrary to the plain character and claims of the book, that the simplest statement of the case ought to be all that is needed to disprove and to discredit it.

For example, in historic facts apart from inconsequent and remote inferences, one great national institution, and only one, was ordained between the death of Moses and the captivity, the magnificent service of song, with symbol, psaltery, and harp, in the worship of the sanctuary; and to this outstanding ordinance the Deuteronomic code, from first to last, makes not the slightest allusion. Whatever, therefore, the object of its author may have been, most certainly nothing was further from his design than to bring down the institutions of the nation from Moses to the time of the later kings.

Again, in the laws of Moses there was one great command, and only one, which at that period had for ever ceased to be in force, and obedience to which would then have been transformed into the worst of crimes, the order for the destruction of the Canaanites. This obsolete order the supposed author of Deuteronomy revives with a sevenfold severity; he repeats it in various sections and in four different chapters of his book, and allots to it a larger space than to all the Ten Commandments. Such legislation is the exact contrary to a development of the laws of Moses so as to adjust them to later times.

Still further, one of the most attractive portions of the more strictly legislative part of the book is the concluding chapter of the central section, in which forms of thanksgiving are provided for Israel in presenting at the sanctuary annual first-fruits, and triennial tithes of the land promised to their fathers, and now enjoyed as their inheritance. These prayers are replete with tenderness and beauty, possessing a special fitness in times of blessing such as those of Joshua and Solomon, while suitable, as prepared by Moses, for all ordinary conditions of the nation; because, except for their own sins, such times would have been abiding. Israel in presenting his offerings before the Lord recalls his national history from the hour when the father of the twelve tribes was still Jacob, just escaped from the land of Syria, and ready to perish, with his wives and children, by the hand of Esau ; and traces it through the bondage and the blessing in Egypt onward to the time of the worshipper, when Israel is in possession of all the land, given by oath to his fathers, and has found the fulfilment equal to the promise of "a land flowing with milk and honey :"

" I profess this day unto the Lord thy God, that I am come unto the country which the Lord sware unto our fathers for to give us. . . . A Syrian ready to perish was my father, and he went down into Egypt, and sojourned there with a few, and became there a nation, great, mighty, and populous : and the Egyptians evil entreated us, and afflicted us, and laid upon us hard bondage : and when we cried unto the Lord God of our fathers, the Lord heard our voice . . . and he hath brought us into this place, and hath given us this land, even a land that floweth with milk and honey. . . . I have hearkened unto the voice of the Lord my God, and have done according to all that thou hast commanded me. Look down from thy holy habitation, from heaven, *and bless thy people Israel, and the land which thou hast given us, as thou swarest unto our fathers,* a land that floweth with milk and honey" (chap. xxvi. 3, 5, 6, 7, 9, 15).

These prayers are expressly given to be used in Israel; but at the period when the new theory holds them to have been written for their use, no words can be conceived more utterly incongruous to the past history or the present condition of the nation. So far was Israel from now possessing the whole land of promise that ten out of the twelve tribes had been disinherited for their transgressions, partly carried away captive by the King of Assyria, and partly left as " an escaped remnant " under a foreign yoke. At such a period no prophet could for the first time have composed this form of prayer for popular use in Israel ; it would have been false in the lips of Judah, and only a national insult to the remnant of Ephraim, whom King Josiah, like Hezekiah before him, was earnestly endeavouring to bring back to the sanctuary of their fathers. Before the discovery of the Book, he had gathered freewill offerings for repairing the Temple from " Manasseh and Ephraim, and from all the remnant of Israel " (2 Chron. xxxiv. 9). Afterwards, in coming up to Jerusalem, to worship in the sanctuary which their gifts had aided to renew, they must have been confounded when there was read in their hearing a new code of ordinances, just sanctioned by the king, in which a prominent place was given to public thanksgiving for Israel's present possession of the whole land of their inheritance. Nothing could have been better fitted to awaken the old jealousy of Ephraim against Judah, and to drive them back to their homes in indignation at having these hypocritical prayers thrust into their lips; as if by lauding their constancy and their prosperity to taunt them with their national declension and degradation. No sanction to prayers, so proud and so meaningless for such a time, could ever have been given by Josiah, whose most seasonable words, after hearing the book of the law, were these, " Go, inquire of the Lord for me, and *for them that are left* in Israel and in Judah."

Should it be arbitrarily alleged that these prayers may have been old words of Moses, which had been left untouched, still, if the design of the new author was to adapt his code to present needs, and " bring it down to date;" and if, in working out this design, he took the liberty of omitting or retaining, supplementing or altering, the words of Moses according to his own judgment, he could most easily have either adapted the prayers to the altered state of the nation, or avoided a direct contradiction to that state. Clearly, there was nothing further from the mind of the author of Deuteronomy than such an adaptation; and these forms of devotion designed for national use in Israel admit of only one explanation, resting on the old and unshaken ground that both the prayers and the book in which they are embodied are the utterances of Moses.

These leading examples make it evident that those who had charge of the Book that was found in the Temple, both before and after its discovery, had scrupulously refrained from adding to, or taking from, the laws of Moses; and from altering them either by the inserted sanction of Divine ordinances that were subsequent to their original enactment, or by the mitigation of severities that were for ever past, or by the remoulding of devotional forms for national use that could no longer express the national mind. At once, by what it omits and what it ordains, the book of Deuteronomy, if of recent date, is the reverse of such an adaptation as the critics have supposed. How men of high intellect and of the amplest learning can have persuaded themselves that this unmanageable theory explains the design of the book, is harder to account for than any difficulties in the book itself; for it wants even the doubtful merit of a clever guess, but is an obvious and a complete mistake. After others have embraced their views to their irreparable loss, and after the faith of many in the Word of God has been shaken with little hope of recovery, they may find themselves constrained to give up their present opinions as untenable; for their own reason in the end will surely crave a likelier theory, with some aspect of reasonableness. Meanwhile, we must be content to defend the truth of the Scriptures with patience and in love; and in the spirit of a Scriptural contention with esteemed brethren, we pursue our examination of this book of Deuteronomy as recording the words of Moses.

CHAPTER I.

ISRAEL'S WITNESS TO MOSES AND TO GOD ON THE PLAINS OF MOAB.

THE Book of Deuteronomy was given to Israel, not only under the form of an historical record, but in the highest and most sacred form in which such a record can be written. In the Scriptures, both Old and New, God has chosen a people, or has elected men, to whom He has said, "Ye are my witnesses;" and has used them to testify with the lips, or to record with the pen, what they have seen and heard. In the history of Israel, from the Red Sea to the Jordan, it has been His good pleasure that our faith in His wondrous works should not rest on the word of Moses alone, but on the testimony of the whole nation by whom they were witnessed; of the chiefs of the tribes, of the elders, of the priests, and of all the people of Israel. For the sake of this attestation, and on the ground of it entering anew into solemn covenant with their God, they were summoned together by their leader on the plains of Moab; who went over in their hearing, not all the details, but the great leading facts of the history through which they had passed, and called them to witness before the Lord in their great national assembly the truth of these events. This he did in various terms throughout his address, both in its earlier and in its later parts (chap. iv. 11, 12, 33-36; chap. xxix. 2-8); and also very fully in what is usually regarded as its legislative portion (chap. v. 23; chap. vi. 21, 22; chap. xi. 2-7). On the ground of what they had themselves seen and heard, he takes them bound by their own express consent to have the Lord for their God, and declares that the Lord owns and claims them for His people: "Thou hast avouched the Lord this day to be thy God; and the Lord hath avouched thee this day to be His peculiar people" (chap. xxvi. 17, 18).

The great lawgiver, while afterwards intimating that this covenant is to descend to future ages (chap. xxix. 14, 15), defines with the most careful precision the one generation of Israel with whom it is now made, expressly excluding other generations, and limiting the partakers in the covenant to those who had witnessed the great works of the Lord:

"Ye came near, and stood under the mountain; and the mountain burned with fire, ... and the Lord spake unto you out of the midst of the fire (chap. iv. 11, 12). The Lord talked with you face to face in the mount out of the midst of the fire (chap. v. 4). And know ye this day, for I speak *not with your children* which have not known, and *which have not seen* the chastisement of the Lord your God, ... and his miracles, and his acts, which he did in the midst of Egypt, ... and what he did unto the army of Egypt, unto their horses and to their chariots; ... and what he did unto Dathan and Abiram: ... how the earth opened her mouth and swallowed them up. ... But *your eyes have seen* all the great acts of the Lord which he did (chap. xi. 2-7). And Moses called unto all Israel, and said unto them, Ye *have seen* all that the Lord did before your eyes in the land of Egypt. ... Ye *stand this day* all of you before the Lord your God; your captains of your tribes, your elders, and your officers, with all the men of Israel; your little ones, your wives, and thy stranger that is in thy camp, from the hewer of thy wood unto the drawer of thy water; *that thou shouldest enter into covenant* with the Lord thy God, and into his oath, which the Lord thy God maketh with thee this day" (chap. xxix. 2, 10-12).

Next to the hearing of the law at the foot of Mount Sinai, this covenant on the plains of Moab is the greatest national transaction in the whole history of Israel; it is a covenant of the Lord with the witnesses of His glory on the mount, of His miracles in Egypt, and of His wondrous works in the desert; a covenant with a divinely disciplined people, blessed and chastened into loyalty to their God, to whom He could say—"Thou shalt remember all the way which the Lord thy God led thee these forty years in the wilderness, to humble thee, and to prove thee : . . . and He fed thee with manna, . . . that He might make thee know that man doth not live by bread alone: . . . thy raiment waxed not old upon thee, neither did thy foot swell, these forty years" (chap. viii. 2, 3, 4). It is the chief witness-bearing given to us of these grand events. Once and again Moses calls on them as witnesses of all they had seen and heard; he rehearses to them the laws (now said to have been enacted seven hundred years after they were dead), which he takes them bound to obey; on the combined grounds of the works of the Lord they had already witnessed, and these statutes they now consented to observe, he declares that they avouched the Lord to be their God (chap. xxvi. 16, 17); he records their testimony and their covenant in the Book of the Law of the Lord, and in their presence delivers the book to the priests to be laid up in the side of the ark (chap. xxxi. 9, 26). This is the most important historical record by eye-witnesses in the Old Testament; and if it is not believed as historically true, nothing else in the Bible can be received as true history, except on the authority of heathen historians. The Bible has given to this transaction the highest and most solemn attestation, Divine and human, of which history is capable; and if so fully attested a record is not historically true, no plea can be made good for the truth of the rest. The historical truth of the entire events recorded in Exodus and the other books must in that case be given up; for the highest attestation given in the Bible to their truth is abandoned, when the Scriptural account of that attestation is held to be fictitious. The most likely reason that could be assigned for the elaborate production of such a fictitious testimony, would be the writer's knowledge that the history of Israel was not authentic, and his desire to confirm it by the highest apparent authority; and any author who could invent the story of the divinely and nationally attested record, would have still less scruple in inventing the historical events themselves.

We are met, however, by the following answer from one of our most distinguished professors:—

"There is not one historical fact of any importance in the history of redemption which the most advanced position of recent critics interferes with. The Egyptian bondage, the Exodus, the Sinaitic covenant, and the occupation of Canaan all remain; nobody doubts them. . . . Deuteronomy is, on any hypothesis, a repetition. It tells a second time the story told before elsewhere. What is lost, if it be not of the age of Moses, is not the truth of the story, but the contemporaneousness of the witness.—And in regard to what is most peculiar and important, the view taken by Israel of the religious meaning of the events of its history, the supernatural light in which it regarded them, this view is not dependent on contemporaneousness or the reverse."*

But if Deuteronomy be not of the age of Moses, what we lose is not the mere contemporaneousness of the witness, but the truth of the entire story, because the narrative professes to have been spoken in the presence of myriads of witnesses contemporaneous with the events; and if there was no truth in their witnessing, we have no ground for trusting the truth of the events. If all that was done and spoken and written on the eastern bank of the Jordan is now

* Old Testament Exegesis in 1878. By Professor Davidson, Edinburgh, D.D., LL.D., p. 23.

discovered to be a mere dramatic representation, composed after many centuries, of events partly real, like the covenant at Sinai, and partly fictitious, like the covenant on the plains of Moab; and if the trusted eye-witnesses were only actors in a drama, the entire history of Moses and of Israel is for ever discredited, because it has no better evidence on which to rest. The statement that the chief facts in the history of redemption are accepted by all the critics does not meet the case, because most of the critics who deny the Mosaic origin of Deuteronomy deny even more positively the miraculous events to which Moses cites Israel as witnesses. It is not the mere history of an exodus and a covenant at Sinai, and a journey through the wilderness to the Jordan, that Moses calls on Israel to testify; but the grand miraculous events, the mighty acts of the Lord in that history which most of these critics utterly deny; and it is a most inadequate account of those miraculous works to say that "Israel regarded them in a supernatural light," when many of them, like the earth swallowing up Dathan and Abiram, not only had "a religious meaning," but had no existence except as supernatural events occurring before their eyes.

It may be added that the character of the testimony is not altered by the fact that in the wilderness "all the people that were men of war which came out of Egypt were consumed." Along with the two leading witnesses, Joshua and Caleb, thousands of grown men under twenty years, with youths of every age growing early into maturity in Egypt, had passed through the Red Sea, had heard the Law at Mount Sinai, and now stood before Moses by the Jordan; whilst all of every age, from the now aged matrons who had brought their children out of Egypt to "the little ones" gathered in the great assembly, had seen more or less of the wonders of the Lord in the desert.

The book of Deuteronomy records Israel's national witnessing to the greatest events in the Old Testament history of redemption; and on the historical truth of this record the truth of the whole Scriptural history evidently rests, for there is no other series of events in Scripture that is attested by so great a cloud of witnesses, and the truth of the attestation is sealed by as many witnesses as the truth of the events.

CHAPTER II.

THE BOOK FOUND IN THE TEMPLE: THE FORM OF DEUTERONOMY NOT DRAMATIC.

ACCORDING to the inspired record, the book that was found in the Temple in the reign of Josiah was either the whole Pentateuch, as seems probable, or one part of the law of Moses—" Hilkiah the priest found a book of the law of the Lord *given* by Moses," or, as in the margin, " by the hand of Moses" (2 Chron. xxxiv. 14). Dr. Kennicott, in his Dissertations, takes this to mean " in the hand of Moses," and maintains that it was the lawgiver's original autograph. But, however this may be, the testimony in Chronicles is quite express that the book that was found was the law of Moses. In the book of Kings it is called simply " The book of the law " (2 Kings xxii. 8); but that the inspired writer means " the book of the law of Moses," he has not left open to doubt, for elsewhere he expressly quotes Deuteronomy as written by Moses : " But the children of the murderers he slew not, according unto that which is written *in the book of the law of Moses*, wherein the Lord commanded, saying, The fathers shall not be put to death for the children, nor the children for the fathers; but every man shall be put to death for his own sin " (2 Kings xiv. 6; Deut. xxiv. 16). One of the sacred historians thus expressly states that the book that was found was the law of Moses, which ought of itself to be sufficient for all who duly reverence the Word of God, and the other quotes at length a statute from Deuteronomy as written in the law of Moses : so that both agree in holding the book found in the Temple to have been the law given by Moses.

Beyond the entirely accordant narratives of the two inspired authors, we know nothing of a book having been found in the Temple at all; and there can be no doubt that if the incident had seemed to be against their views, the rationalists after their wonted manner would have discredited the entire story as not probable and therefore not historical, but added traditionally by later writers. They employ it, however, as the one great support of their theory; yet most irrationally they believe and magnify the narrative, so far as they can interpret it in their own favour; but otherwise they absolutely reject it, because it simply destroys their whole theory. The Bible states that a book of the law, or the book of the law, by the hand of Moses, was found in the Temple, which they deny because Deuteronomy would then be the law of Moses. But they affirm, on the sole authority of the Bible, that a book was found in the Temple; that is, they believe this fact without any ground for their belief except the very authority which they disbelieve. If they had some authority outside the Bible for what they receive and for what they reject, they might have a plea of reason, although none of faith; but there is no reason in believing the Scripture when it writes that a book was found, and in disbelieving it when it writes that it was the law of Moses that was found. So irrational in this, as in many instances, is rationalistic criticism.

Of the theory that finds a new code of laws in the book found in the Temple, the only plausible form is the original one of the rationalists ascribing it to a pious fraud. That the old book of the law should have been found in the recesses of the Temple was natural enough. But that a new code of laws should have been discovered there is a story that can bear telling only on the supposition that it was concealed so as to be found through them by whom it had been hidden on purpose that it might be taken for an old book of Moses, as it evidently was by the king and all the nation, who regarded it with the highest possible reverence. But such a fraud would exclude it from a place in the Holy Scriptures; and is rejected by those amongst ourselves who deny the Mosaic origin of the book in favour of another theory, which must be regarded as both more unlikely in history, and worse in morals.

To remove the insuperable difficulty of fraud, it has been held that the recent origin of the book was openly stated, and publicly recognised; but that a Mosaic authority was claimed for its repetition of the history of Israel, and its supplementary code of laws. In that case the national assembly, to whom the book was read, concurred in an unparalleled deception on all ages to come, by sanctioning its insertion in the holiest records of the nation under the revered name of Moses. That assembly, convened by the king, consisted of "all the elders of Judah and Jerusalem, . . . the priests and the prophets, and all the people, both small and great;" and they "made a covenant before the Lord, to walk after the Lord, and to keep his commandments and his testimonies and his statutes with all their heart and all their soul, to perform the words of this covenant that were written in this book" (2 Kings xxiii. 3). The book and the covenant to which they stood before the Lord bore this title, "These be the words which Moses spake unto all Israel, on this side Jordan, in the land of Moab;" as such Josiah and his people accepted it for themselves, as such they transmitted it to their children, and as such it has been received by their descendants to this day. But by the new theory the whole nation, engaging in these solemn transactions before the Lord, handed down to all generations of mankind a book of their own days as the work of their great lawgiver and prophet seven hundred years before. The trembling king and his humbled people listened to the astounding effrontery of the assertion, that the words read in their ears were spoken to the generation who had passed through the Red Sea and the wilderness, and neither to their fathers before, nor to their children after (chap. v. 3; xi. 2); and knowing that they were themselves the first assembly that had ever heard them, they consented that such a book should be laid up in the oracles of God as addressed to Israel of old by Moses himself! The fraud of a single false prophet deceiving the people would have been a far lighter crime; for his would have been the sin of one man, and theirs the sin of the whole nation. Such are the impossible suppositions involved in these ill-considered speculations.

The Form of Deuteronomy not Dramatic.—Before the rise of recent modern criticism, one of the objections against Moses, as the author of Deuteronomy, was taken from the immaterial circumstance that he speaks of himself as Moses, whence the inference was drawn that the book was written of him and not by him—"*non a Mose, sed de Mose.*" Afterwards, at the close of last century, in his "Age of Reason," Thomas Paine, who believed indeed in God as his Creator and Judge, but had a fierce hatred to the Bible (except the Book of Job and the nineteenth Psalm, which he highly extols), in seeking to disprove the authenticity of Deuteronomy, as of the other books, took up at some length this objection to Moses writing of himself in the third person. He supposes the book to have been written three or four hundred years after the death of Moses, and represents the author as composing it after the manner of a drama, and introducing Moses once and again as a speaker. With the natural vigour of his intellect, not strained by critical studies, he held it as certain, that if he could disprove its antiquity and Mosaic authority, all its claim to inspiration would be gone. But it was answered that for a writer to speak of himself in the third person was a form employed by the best ancient authors. That it was used by Moses himself is clear from his summary of Israel's journeyings near the end of the preceding book of Numbers. In the beginning of the thirty-third chapter we read: "These are the journeys of the children of Israel, which went forth out of the land of Egypt with their armies under the hand of Moses and Aaron. And Moses wrote their goings out according to their journeys by the commandment of the Lord: and these are their journeys according to their goings out" (v. 1, 2). Then follow the exact words of Moses, which he wrote by the command of God (v. 3). But he does not write as we might have expected, "And *we* departed from Rameses in the first month," but "And *they* departed," and so throughout the chapter; speaking of the progress of the nation as "their goings," and not as "ours," although all the while he was himself their leader. But to modern ears, as well to ancient, if we mistake not, the form which the Hebrew lawgiver has adopted in his introduction to the noble record of the nation's history and teaching and laws is preferable to any other. "These are the words which I spake unto all Israel on this side Jordan in the wilderness" would even to us have been neither so good nor so natural a title for his great work as the one which he has himself preferred: "These are the words which Moses spake unto all Israel on this side Jordan in the wilderness." The other instances follow naturally in the same form.

CHAPTER III.

THIS OTHER SIDE OF JORDAN.

THAT the Hebrew lawgiver in the record of his address should introduce it as having been spoken by Moses, cannot well be numbered even amongst apparent difficulties; but with this objection another was raised which is at first sight startling, if Deuteronomy is read without reference to the preceding books. It was objected that the expression in our English Bible, "on this side Jordan" in the first verse, ought to have been "on the other side of Jordan;" but the objection was sufficiently answered two centuries ago on the incontrovertible ground that the expression is used for the same side as that of the speaker as well as for the opposite.

Amongst ourselves, however, it has now acquired an unexpected importance; for it has lately been repeated in a very decided form by a critic whose eminence in Hebrew and thorough knowledge of the subjects he handles and habitual caution entitle his statement to the most deferential and careful consideration:—

"The very first verse of Deuteronomy reads properly thus: 'These are the words which Moses spake unto all Israel on the *other side* of Jordan.' Here Moses, on the supposition that he wrote this verse, names the land of Moab, where he stood, the other side of Jordan. . . . The very phrase 'the other side of Jordan' is one which, in his day, had not arisen. It is due to the occupation of Canaan by Israel as a fact. . . . It is more probable that this verse belongs to a later writer."—(Professor Davidson's *Old Test. Exegesis*, p. 17.)

The use by Moses of the phrase "the other side of Jordan" is here held to be improbable; it is positively stated to have arisen only after the occupation of Canaan; and we take for granted that the substance of the phrase is meant, and not any slight variation, as in English we might say either "on the other side," or "at the other side." It must certainly be allowed that not "this side," but "the other side of Jordan" is the literal translation; but the supposition that Moses was not likely to have employed the expression is without foundation, and the statement that it arose only after the occupation of Canaan by Israel is against all evidence. In the time of Moses it appears to have been the recognised designation of the country; and no other term is known by which he could have described it except the still more definite one, "the other side of Jordan toward the sun-rising," which might hastily be taken to indicate even more strongly the position of a writer on the western side of the river. Let us look first at the meaning of the expression as in use by Israel, and then as used by Moses himself.

1. *The meaning of the term as in use by Israel before the passage of the Jordan.*—As regards its date the origin of the expression remains unknown, but the most natural conclusion is, that it took its rise when the patriarchs dwelt in the land of Canaan. The entire home of their sojourn, the land through which they were to walk, "in the length of it and in the breadth of it," was the land of Canaan; and to them as well as to Israel, after their settlement under Joshua, the land of Bashan and Gilead was on the other side of Jordan. It was after he had crossed the Jordan into the land of Canaan that God said to Abraham, "Unto thy seed will I give this land;" and in all his wide wanderings within and without the promised inheritance, and despite of the attractiveness of the pastures in Bashan and Gilead, he never recrossed the Jordan with his herds and flocks. Isaac all his lifetime never pitched his tent east of the Jordan, and by his father's command he did not cross it even to fetch his bride to her new home. Jacob speaks as if he had counted himself an exile from the central land of promise all the while that he lived on the other side of the Jordan; for on reaching its eastern bank on his return, he says, "With my staff I passed over this Jordan," or came to its further side. His son Joseph passed his youth in Canaan, and the space of an ordinary life would bridge over the period between his death and the birth of Moses. To Moses himself the eastern land must always have been "the other side of Jordan," from the land of special promise; for he appears to have had no intention of occupying it, but courteously asked Sihon for liberty to pass through his country across the Jordan into the land of Canaan.

In the patriarchal times, however, there is no record of the use of the term, for "the threshing-floor of Atad, which is on the other side of Jordan" (Gen. l. 10, 11), is a description by Moses and not by Joseph, and the site of Atad has been disputed. After the exodus, when Moses writes in the 22nd chapter of Numbers (v. 1), "The children of Israel set forward and pitched in the plains of Moab *on the other side of Jordan* by Jericho," our translators render it "on this side Jordan by Jericho;" and their reason for taking this liberty evidently was that to us the other side means the side opposite to the speaker or writer, while Moses was himself on the same side of Jordan which he calls the other side. The difficulty might have been rather better solved by retaining "other," by marking "this" as an insertion of their own, and by translating "The children of Israel pitched in the plains of Moab on *this* other side of Jordan by Jericho."

The necessity for such a modification of the original phrase is very evident in the thirty-second chapter of the same book, where, according to the correction contended for, the 19th verse ought to have not "on this side," but "on the other side." By such a translation we should preserve the Hebrew idiom at the cost of divesting the passage of any intelligible meaning to all but one out of a hundred readers. In the clear language of our English Bible, the tribes of Gad and Reuben say to Moses on the plains of Moab, "We will not inherit with them *on yonder side Jordan*, or forward; because our inheritance is fallen to us *on this side Jordan* eastward." But in a closely literal translation of their own words these tribes say: "We will not inherit with them *on the other side of Jordan*, or forward; because our inheritance is fallen to us *on the other side of Jordan* eastward." Here the first "other side of Jordan" is so called for the evident reason that the west bank of the river was opposite to the camp of Israel; but the second "other side" is the bank on which they are encamped, and their reason for giving it such a designation must certainly have been that it was the common name of the district of country. This inconvenient employment of the appellation in the very sentence in which they had applied the same term to the opposite side of the river shows that it could not well be dispensed with by the substitution of any other name; and that it had been so well established and was in such familiar use among the people as to overcome the otherwise serious unseasonableness of the repetition.

In the 32nd verse of the same chapter, "the other side," instead of "this side" would convey a clear enough sense; but unhappily that sense would not convey the truth but its direct contrary, for the English expression would denote the land of Canaan on the west side of the river opposite to Israel: "We will pass over armed before the Lord into the land of Canaan, that the possession of our inheritance *on the other side of Jordan* may be ours." If what the readers of our Bible want is not Hebrew but English, and if one of the designs of a translation is to convey the meaning of the original, and not its mere idiom, the critical emendation would in this instance amount to a serious mistranslation of the text, the meaning of which is at once distinct and true in our English Bible: "We will pass over armed before the Lord into the land of Canaan, that the possession of our inheritance *on this side Jordan* may be ours;" or "on *this* other side of Jordan" might be still better.

In addressing these same tribes after the death of Moses, before Israel had crossed the Jordan, Joshua, while recalling the words of Moses, twice over in his own words uses the term "other side" to denote its eastern bank:—

"Remember the word which Moses the servant of the Lord commanded you, saying, the Lord hath given you rest, and hath given you *this* land. Your wives, your little ones, and your cattle, shall remain in the land which Moses gave you *on this side Jordan;* . . . then shall ye return unto the land of your possession, . . . which Moses the Lord's servant gave you *on this side Jordan* toward the sun-rising" (Josh. i. 13-15).

If critics prefer to retain the Hebrew idiom, and to translate "the land which Moses gave you on the other side of Jordan," they must of necessity add a marginal explanation that the reader is to understand "*this* other side," or to bear in mind that it does *not* mean the other side from that on which Joshua was standing, but the *same* side, which in ordinary English is "this side."

2. *The meaning of the term as used by Moses.*—Limiting our inquiry, as in these preceding passages, to words spoken in the first person, and therefore not open to any suggestion of being later explanations, we read in the thirty-fourth chapter of Numbers (ver. 13-15)—

"And Moses commanded the children of Israel, saying, This is the land which ye shall inherit by lot, which the Lord commanded to give unto the nine tribes, and to the half tribe: for the tribe of the children of Reuben, . . . and the tribe of the children of Gad: . . . the two tribes and the half tribe have received their inheritance *on the other side Jordan* near Jericho eastward, toward the sun-rising."

If these words are read apart from any preceding context, like the introduction to Deuteronomy, they will be accepted without hesitation as intimating that Moses is in the land of Canaan, which he is giving to the nine tribes and a-half, and that he speaks of the eastern bank of the Jordan as "the other side" from that on which he stands, but nothing is further from his meaning; and to prevent so great a misconception our authorised translation is, "They have received their inheritance *on this side*," as in the introduction to Deuteronomy, and for the same reason.

In the 35th chapter, again, we read (ver. 9, 14)—

"The Lord spake unto Moses, saying, Speak unto the children of Israel, and say unto them, When ye be come over Jordan into the land of Canaan . . . ye shall give three cities *on the other side of Jordan*, and three cities ye shall give in the land of Canaan, which shall be cities of refuge."

In these words the second injunction seems to be a mere repetition of the first, because the land of Canaan was on "the other side of Jordan" from the camp of Israel; and our translators, at the expense of the Hebrew idiom, have given the true meaning, "three cities *on this side Jordan*, and three in the land of Canaan."

Once more, in the 3rd chapter of Deuteronomy (ver. 8), Moses says—

"We took at that time out of the hand of the two kings of the Amorites the land that was *on the other side of Jordan*, from the river of Arnon unto Mount Hermon."

The introduction to the book informs us that in speaking these words Moses stood in the land of Moab, and here he definitely describes the neighbouring kingdoms of Sihon and of Og as "*on the other side of Jordan*" when speaking of them as on the same side of Jordan with Israel and himself. Evidently this was the natural, the recognised, and apparently the only general term by which Moses could describe that Eastern land; and our translators, if they would not mislead their readers, held themselves obliged to sacrifice the Hebrew idiom for the sake of the true meaning, and to say "the land that was *on this side Jordan*, from the river of Arnon unto Mount Hermon."

Therefore, when finally, in the opening of Deuteronomy, Moses was describing the place where he then stood, there is no doubt that he would call it "the other side of Jordan," as the name of that land by use and wont, as the name by which he was himself in the habit of calling it, and as the name by which it was known in Israel whom he was about to address. So far, indeed, is the expression from being confined to the period of Israel's history after the passage of the Jordan, recorded in Joshua, that if we include Deuteronomy and take into account the disparity in size of the two portions of the Old Testament, its use is rather more frequent before than after it. Its occurrence in the beginning of Deuteronomy is entirely accordant with Moses having written the introduction, as well as the rest of the book; and the expression, which cannot be taken as an evidence either way, is not against the Mosaic authorship, but rather in its favour.

In the end of the 4th chapter there are four additional instances which we have not included, because being in the third person they will not be allowed by most of those who deny the introduction to Moses. But to those who accept the book as written by him they will serve to confirm his writing of the introduction; and they are all translated "on this side Jordan."

"Then Moses severed three cities *on this side Jordan* toward the sun-rising; these are the testimonies which Moses spake *on this side Jordan;* they possessed his land and the land of Og *on this side Jordan* toward the sun-rising; and all the plain *on this side Jordan* eastward" (Deut. iv. 41, 46, 47, 49).

On the subsequent use of the term we only remark that Israel, after they had crossed the river, still occasionally called Canaan "the other side," because opposite to the land they had lately left (Josh. v. 1; ix. 1; xii. 1); or even because opposite to the land to which they were chiefly referring at the time (Josh. xxii. 7; 1 Chron. xxvi. 30, 32). But alike before and after their occupation of Canaan "The Other Side of Jordan" was the proper idiomatic designation of the eastern side of the river. In the words of another, "such phrases get to be current idioms of language, wherever geographically they are used: as modern writers speak of Cisalpine Gaul, or of Ultramontane tenets, whether the speaker be in Rome, Geneva, or London."

The argument may be put very briefly in another form. The plea against the first verse of Deuteronomy being the utterance of Moses is, that its terms, "These be the words which Moses spake on the other side of Jordan," indicate an author in the land of Canaan speaking of the eastern bank of the river as its "other side." But in the 8th verse of the 3rd chapter, Moses himself uses the very same phrase in the sense of "this other side" for the eastern bank on which he stands: "We took at that time the land that was on the other side of Jordan . . .

this land which we possessed at that time" (ver. 12). Now, on the one hand, if Moses really speaks in the 8th verse of the 3rd chapter, there is no reason to hold that he does not also speak in the 1st verse of the 1st chapter, because the language is exactly the same. But if, on the other hand, the whole is the work of a later author, the fact of his putting "the other side of Jordan" into the lips of Moses in the 3rd chapter in the sense of "this other side," is a sufficient ground for inferring that it is used in the same sense in the opening of the book; and most assuredly the expression, as coming from the pen of this alleged writer, can never be proved to mean "that other side of Jordan."

This inquiry into a subject that has become unexpectedly important establishes these results : That in the time of Moses "The Other Side of Jordan" bore very much the character of a proper name for a general designation of the land on the east of the river; that this designation was used by speakers on the eastern side of the river quite as freely and as correctly as on its western side; that no other general term is known by which Moses could have designated that land, and that this one he used repeatedly; that in an introduction to an address on the plains of Moab, it is the very term he was certain to employ for describing the position of Israel and his own; that the plea against the introduction to Deuteronomy having been written by Moses on the ground of its being an expression he could not have used is without foundation; and that in these introductory verses, the only reasonable, and in the highest degree probable interpretation of the term would be thus expressed : "These be the words which Moses spake unto all Israel on (this) other side of Jordan, in the wilderness; on (this) other side of Jordan, in the land of Moab, began Moses to declare this law."*

---

* Professor Smith's view, which agrees with Dr. Davidson's, has long been before the public, and is repeated in the Answer to the Amended Libel (p. 6): "The very first verse of Deuteronomy says, 'These be the words which Moses spake unto all Israel *across the Jordan* in the wilderness;' and this is not a solitary proof that the book, as we possess it, was written down *after* the people had entered into possession of Canaan."

CHAPTER IV.

THEORY OF A NEW CODE IN THE HEART OF AN OLD BOOK.

THE consideration of Professor Smith's last explanatory statement was not in the design of this brief treatise, of which a great part had been written previously. The restricted theory he now maintains is not that recentness of Deuteronomy which Professor Davidson seems to defend without adopting; but some notice of it is necessary, else the true matter of discussion might seem to be avoided, whilst the publication of his statement in a separate form indicates his own desire to have the subject reasoned out by all interested in it.

Professor Smith states:

"My remarks apply to the legal part of the book as it once existed apart from the history, and this separate publication is the book which I speak of as 'a prophetic legislative programme,' and identify with the written law-book that guided Josiah in his reformations" (p. 9). "Josiah, as every one admits, had that law in his hand, and thereafter we find it well known to Jeremiah. Does not this seem to show that the new law was revealed sometime between Isaiah and Jeremiah, in order to give practical effect to the teaching of the former prophet and his helpers?" (p. 13).

He offers two forms of this legislative portion of Deuteronomy, a larger and a lesser, and sometimes expresses no preference for either:

"The original book may have begun with the superscription, iv. 44, or only with xii. 1. It may have ended with the peroration, xxvi. 16-19, or with the subscription, xxix. 1" (p. 9). "I believe that the laws of Deut. xii.-xxvi. were originally published *either alone* [the italics are ours] or with the introductory address in chaps. v.-xi. as a preface, and, perhaps, some part of xxvii., xxviii. as a conclusion" (p. 29).

But when a preference is indicated, it is rather for that section of the book to which he seems to lean, in the words we have marked in the following sentence :—

"It is generally held by critics, and it is my own opinion, that the statement of the law in the heart of the book (that is, chaps. v. to xxvi., or *rather, perhaps, only chaps.* xii.-xxvi.) was once published in a separate form as a practical manual for popular use, and existed in that form for some time before it was incorporated in that great body of mingled history and law which we call the Pentateuch" (p. 8).

The limitation of the theory to these fifteen chapters is also the form which his friends accept as presenting its most favourable aspect; while the wider supposition denies to Moses so very large a portion of the book, and, as regards the main line of argument and most of its details, is so nearly equivalent to the denial of the whole, as not to call for a separate consideration, which would involve a large repetition of the same arguments. This wider theory is not at all given up, and is expressly retained in case it should be preferred in the end; but as, by making the recent code to consist of chapters iv. 44 to xxix. 1, it takes from Moses nearly three-fourths of what, on the face of it, pertains to him (twenty-four chapters out of thirty-three), the authorship of the rest becomes a very small matter to all who hold the integrity of the Word of God. Whether the remaining fourth part is assigned to Moses or to another can never be a subject of importance, or even of interest, to the Church.

Confining our attention, therefore, for the present, to the theory in its restriction to chapters xii. to xxvi., it is difficult to see how it has been supposed that even this narrowest limitation simplifies or improves the case; and the interpolation of a book of fictitious historical legislation in the heart of a book of genuine history would be, in one view, even a greater corruption of the record, and more injurious to its Divine authority, than an entire book of fiction under the guise of authentic history.

The verse preceding the interpolation is "Ye shall observe to do all the statutes and judgments which I (Moses) set before you this day" (chap. xi. 32); the opening words of the code are, "These are the statutes and judgments, which ye shall observe to do in the land, which the Lord God of thy fathers giveth thee" (chap. xii. 1), and it proceeds, "For ye are not as yet come to the rest and to the inheritance which the Lord your God giveth you" (ver. 9). In closing the code, Moses recurs to the concluding words of the previous section, and says, "This day the Lord thy God hath commanded thee to do these statutes and judgments" (chap. xxvi. 16); and the words immediately following the code are, "And Moses with the elders of Israel commanded the people, saying, Keep all the commandments which I command you this day" (chap. xxvii. 1). The code is thus expressly engrafted into the narrative as given by Moses before crossing the Jordan.

But the interpolated code itself embodies in substance all the evils complained of in the fictitious book. It contains the worst instance of personation in the whole book, and a quite incredible utterance from the lips of an honest man, in the prediction by Moses of "a Prophet like unto me" (chap. xviii. 15); it omits the only great enactment in Israel between Moses and Josiah, the ordinance of praise; it enforces the obsolete ban of extermination against the original inhabitants of the land (chap. xx. 16); it prescribes a new form of thanksgiving by the "people Israel" for the gift and inheritance of the whole land, after ten of their twelve tribes had been disinherited (chap. xxvi. 15); and it finally embodies, as formally as any other section of the book, what to many minds is the crowning scandal of the fictitious transaction of a solemn national covenant between Israel and God, and between God and Israel, on the express footing of this code, which was issued seven hundred years after the death of the covenanting elders and people :

"*This day* the Lord thy God hath commanded thee to do *these statutes and judgments*. . . . Thou hast avouched the Lord *this day* to be thy God, . . . and to keep his statutes, and his commandments, and his judgments : . . . and the Lord hath avouched thee *this day* to be his peculiar people" (chap. xxvi. 16, 17, 18).

The limitation is thus of no value whatever in removing the objections to the theory, which in this restricted form is quite as fatal to the integrity and authority of the Holy Scriptures as if the whole book were held to be fictitious.

But further, if the central code "alone" is accepted as one of the probable or possible forms of this theory, the story of the separate book is impossible, whether it be taken as the very book found by Hilkiah, or as already absorbed in Deuteronomy before its discovery. The only reasonable supposition is that the book at its first discovery existed in its original separate form; but it would be an obvious and extreme mistake to identify the central code with the book that was read by Josiah, for he trembled for "all the curses written" in it against his place and people, and in the fifteen chapters of the code *there is not one specific curse* or *judgment* either on the land or on the nation. While this supposition is plainly impossible, the only other supposition, that the separate book had been absorbed in Deuteronomy before its discovery, would soar quite out of the region of history and criticism, creating the story of the birth, life, and death of a distinct book before there is any trace of its existence. Apart, however, from this difficulty, the conjecture that the code of chapters xii.-xxvi. either did exist, or may have once existed as a separate book, is incompatible with the history of the age, and contrary to all true criticism. The theory maintains that the code was first issued in its complete form between the death of Isaiah and the prophecies of Jeremiah. But if in this code we select a special statute, it is unaccountable that the previous law by Moses in Leviticus should have pronounced the judgment of stoning, under the severest Divine anger, against the man who made his children pass through the fire to Molech (Lev. xx. 1-5); and that a law, issued at a time when this sin was defiling and rapidly destroying the land, should pronounce no judgment at all against the prevalent crime, but merely give the command, "There shall not be found among you any one that maketh his son or his daughter to pass through the fire" (Deut. xviii. 10).

But more generally, the code itself is not a mere body of laws for the regulation of personal life; but it enjoins the great national feasts, ordains the appointment of judges in the cities and the selection of cities of refuge, commands the utter destruction of a city apostatising to idolatry and the extinction of Amalek, gives direction concerning the election of a king, and issues other ordinances that concern the whole nation, such as the proclamation to be issued on the eve of battle. Further, the code does not consist of mere dry enactments; its concluding chapter, as already noted, consists mainly of forms of thanksgiving for the full possession of the land; and the whole is intermingled with blessings, both personal and national. These are some of the blessings :—

"Observe and hear all these words which I command thee, that it may go well with thee, and with thy children after thee for ever (chap. xii. 28). Save when there shall be no poor among you; for the Lord shall greatly bless thee in the land which the Lord thy God giveth thee. . . . For the Lord thy God blesseth thee, as he promised thee: and thou shalt lend unto many nations, but thou shalt not borrow; and thou shalt reign over many nations, but they shall not reign over thee. . . . Thou shalt open thine hand wide unto him (thy poor brother) : . . . because that for this thing the Lord thy God shall bless thee in all thy works, and in all that thou puttest thine hand unto (chap. xv. 4, 6, 8, 10). Because the Lord thy God shall bless thee in all thine increase, and in all the works of thine hands ; therefore thou shalt surely rejoice (chap. xvi. 15). The Lord hath avouched thee this day to be his peculiar people, as he hath promised thee, and that thou shouldest keep all his commandments ; and to make thee high above all nations which he hath made, in praise, and in name, and in honour" (chap. xxvi. 18, 19).

By the side of these national and personal promises and blessings, we have the singular and most striking fact that there is not found a single national curse or judgment or specific threatening from first to last in all these fifteen chapters. The only instance in which the thought of the Divine anger against the nation is introduced is not in the way of threatening, but of showing how the indignation may be turned aside by a righteous people, and end in a blessing, not by repentance, but by faithfulness. In the case of murder, with the guilt untraced, the elders of the city were to wash their hands over a slain heifer, and attest their innocence, and " the blood was to be forgiven them." So with an apostate city, the guilt of idolatry would have involved the whole nation in the anger of the Lord against the city ; but after the faithful execution of judgment upon it, we read—" There shall cleave nought of the cursed thing to thine hand : that the Lord may turn from the fierceness of his anger, and show thee mercy, and have compassion upon thee, and multiply thee, as he hath sworn unto thy fathers" (chap. xiii. 17); the Lord multiplying the faithful nation, so as more than to compensate the loss of the apostate city. Of national warnings there is nothing stronger than the words, " Take heed to thyself that thou be not snared by following them" (the idolatrous nations) (chap. xii. 30). Of personal penalties for transgression there are many ; but all of them are to be inflicted at the hand of Israel, as in the case of the idolatrous prophet or friend or city (chap. xiii.); and in " eye for eye, foot for foot, and hand for hand." The personal threatenings from God directly are that He will require it of the man who will not hearken to the great Prophet, and of him who fails to pay his vow ; and that it will be sin to the man who hardens his heart against his poor brother (chap. xviii. 19; xxiii. 21; xv. 9 ; xxiv. 15).

This portion of Deuteronomy thus contains the very greatest national blessings on Israel immediately from the hand of God; some of them, and in one sense all of them, promises on the condition of obedience; but some of them also so including the implied gift of obedience as to take the form of a promise that could not fail; and its closing chapter teaches Israel how to give thanks for their full possession of the "land flowing with milk and honey" (chap. xxvi.) At the same time, it contains no national curse or judgment or specific threatening for national disobedience; but is all addressed as if to a faithful nation that will execute the judgments of the Lord against the man or the city that is in transgression. If the nation itself should depart from the Lord, no judgment whatever is uttered against it, while in promised blessings it is exalted above all the nations of the earth.

The Word of God in our hands makes it clear that, in accordance with the Divine dealings with the nation, a legislative book of so exclusive a character could never have been given to Israel. In the days of Joshua, of David, and of Solomon these promises were in a great measure fulfilled and these blessings bestowed, and never since; but the book of the law that contained them abounded also in Divine threatenings and judgments and curses, both personal and national, against disobedience; and it is a groundless conception that the portion of Deuteronomy from the 12th to the 26th chapters could have been published by itself to Israel under Divine sanction at any period of the national history.

But the time of that history in which this book is conjectured to have been issued is of all others the period, from the exodus to the destruction of Jerusalem, in which the gift of such a book of blessing would have been utterly unseasonable and deceptive; because it is the period when the iniquity of the nation had become full, when the ten tribes had already been delivered by the Divine indignation into the hand of their enemies, and when the doom of Jerusalem was nearly, if not already sealed. Before the time of its conjectured publication, Isaiah and Micah had uttered judgments of desolation on Jerusalem for her sins; after it Jeremiah repeated the same denunciations; and during it the sins of the nation had reached such a crisis that neither Manasseh's own repentance nor Josiah's reformation could avert its doom. That such a book, promising the largest national blessings without one judgment against a nation sunk in corruption, should have been issued under Divine authority at such a period is incredible and impossible. The historical conjecture, that the central code of Deuteronomy may have been issued by itself as a separate book "*some time between Isaiah and Jeremiah*" is an extreme anachronism.

CHAPTER V.

ISRAEL'S SERVICE OF SONG.

THE Divine institution of the Service of Song by David under his own name furnishes a clear proof that the highest authority in Israel could not invest a new ordinance with a Mosaic sanction; and the absence in Deuteronomy of all reference to this service proves that it was not the design of the book to bring down the institutions of Israel to the time of the later prophets, whilst in a code of such a date under Mosaic sanction the omission would have abolished the existing ordinance.

1. The constant ascription of the great institution of vocal and instrumental praise in the Temple, not to Moses, but to David, proves that there was no power in Israel, priestly, prophetical, or regal, invested with authority to add new laws in the name of Moses. The words of the covenant which Joshua wrote in the book of the law of God were not added in the name of Moses (Joshua xxiv. 26); nor "the manner of the kingdom, which Samuel wrote in a book, and laid up before the Lord" (1 Sam. x. 25). It is no answer to say that the code read to Josiah might have Divine authority to that effect, when the Scripture states that this code was the law of Moses; and the question is, what authority in Israel could make it part of that law, if it was not so in reality? The unknown prophetic author, Hilkiah the priest, and Josiah the king are all conceived to have combined to invest it with an authority not only of Divine sanction, but equal to that of Israel's great and only lawgiver. After Moses, there is no lawgiver and no added code of laws; and, with the single exception of David, there is no authority ever recognised in Israel as entitled to establish any sacred institution, while the lesser authority of David is most carefully distinguished from the higher authority of Moses, which stands always alone. Beyond all

question, if the Divine sanction had been given to a new code of laws, it would have been stated that the book was by the hand of its prophetic author, or of Hilkiah, or of Josiah, or of them all, just as it is said that the service of song was by David along with the prophet Nathan, and Gad the king's seer. Yet there is not the slightest notice of such authority having been given to any of them, or to any other king or prophet, except to David and his prophetic counsellors. The supposition is therefore contrary to all Scriptural history. No mere prophet made laws for Israel, and no mere ruler, and no mere prophet and mere ruler acting together. Moses, the one lawgiver, was both prophet and ruler; and David, who added sacred ordinances, was both prophet and ruler; inferior to Moses, for those ordinances had the added sanction of Gad and Nathan, yet like him in having his institutions honoured as " by the commandment of David, the man of God," as the law was " the law of Moses, the man of God."

The institution of praise was a magnificent one, for which David set apart four thousand Levites; it was before the nation morning and evening in the daily sacrifices of the Temple, and it occupied a prominent place in the great national feasts. It was in full harmony with Mosaic principles, for the Levitical praise with cymbal, psaltery, and harp was a development of the music of the two silver trumpets sounded by the priests over the sacrifices; and Israel had also raised their loud song of praise at the Red Sea, although the further development in the service of song in the sanctuary was entirely new. For its own sake the whole Davidic ordinance of praise deserved the highest national sanction that could be conferred it; on and for its author's sake it had a far higher claim to that sanction than any subsequent institution.

Now, in the prefatory and historical portion of his noble book Moses had expressly said, " Ye shall not add to the word which I (Moses) command you " (chap. iv. 2); not denying that God might sanction other ordinances, but commanding that nothing was ever to be added to the laws of Moses, which were to stand always in their own lofty isolation. The supposed author of the central code, whom we may denounce without malice since he possesses only an imaginary existence, has in the teeth of this imperative command the unequalled audacity to repeat the injunction in the very act of disobeying it; and to write, "What thing soever I (Moses) command you, observe to do it; thou shalt not add thereto" (chap. xii. 32), thus turning the Holy Word of

God into foolishness. But it was by Moses himself that the command was solemnly doubled, because his God would have none ever to speak in his name.

Accordingly, in the Holy Scriptures there is a watchful jealousy to separate the great ordinance of Praise in the most marked way from the institutions of Moses. In connection with the tabernacle or the temple, we have the record of the worship of praise under seven rulers of Israel, and in all of them without exception the ordinance is expressly ascribed to David; guarding it against its being nameless, and so unauthorised, but equally guarding it from ever being attributed to Moses. Not only so, but in each of these instances the name of Moses is in some part of the narrative expressly introduced as the author of his own laws; the things that belong to each being carefully assigned to each. Under Jehoiada we have the following striking example of this jealous care: "Jehoiada appointed the offices of the house of the Lord by the hand of the Levites, whom David had distributed in the house of the Lord, to offer the burnt-offerings of the Lord, as it is written in the law of Moses, with rejoicing and with singing, *as it was ordained* by David" (2 Chron. xxiii. 18). In this relation the whole record is so instructive, that we are induced to give in order all the rulers under whom the offering of praise is recorded in connection with the sanctuary.

DAVID.

Moses.	David.
"And the children of the Levites bare the ark of God upon their shoulders with the staves thereon, as Moses commanded according to the word of the Lord" (1 Chron. xv. 15).	"And David spake to the chief of the Levites to appoint their brethren to be the singers with instruments of musick, psalteries and harps and cymbals, sounding, by lifting up the voice with joy" (ver. 16).

SOLOMON.

"Then Solomon offered burnt-offerings unto the Lord on the altar of the Lord, which he had built before the porch, even after a certain rate every day, offering according to the commandment of Moses" (2 Chron. viii. 12, 13).	"And he appointed, according to the order of David his father, the courses of the priests to their service, and the Levites to their charges, to praise and minister before the priests: ... for so had David the man of God commanded" (ver. 14).

JOASH.

MOSES.	DAVID.
"Also Jehoiada appointed the offices of the house of the Lord by the hand of the priests the Levites, whom David had distributed in the house of the Lord, to offer the burnt-offerings of the Lord, as it is written in the law of MOSES;	with rejoicing and with singing, as it was ordained by DAVID" (2 Chron. xxiii. 18).

HEZEKIAH.

"And they stood in their place after their manner, according to the law of MOSES the man of God: the priests sprinkled the blood, which they received of the hand of the Levites" (2 Chron. xxx. 16).	"And he set the Levites in the house of the Lord with cymbals, with psalteries, and with harps, according to the commandment of DAVID, and of Gad the king's seer, and Nathan the prophet: for so was the commandment of the Lord by his prophets. . . . And when the burnt-offering began, the song of the Lord began also with the trumpets, and with the instruments ordained by DAVID king of Israel" (2 Chron. xxix. 25, 27).

JOSIAH.

"So kill the passover, and sanctify yourselves, and prepare your brethren, that they may do according to the word of the Lord by the hand of MOSES" (2 Chron. xxxv. 6). "And they removed the burnt-offerings, that they might give according to the divisions of the families of the people, to offer unto the Lord, as it is written in the book of MOSES" (ver. 12).	"Prepare yourselves by the houses of your fathers, after your courses, according to the writing of DAVID king of Israel, and according to the writing of Solomon his son" (ver. 4). "And the singers the sons of Asaph were in their place, according to the commandment of DAVID, and Asaph, and Heman, and Jeduthun the king's seer" (ver. 15).

ZERUBBABEL.

"Then stood up Jeshua . . . and builded the altar of the God of Israel, to offer burnt-offerings thereon, as it is written in the law of MOSES the man of God" (Ezra iii. 2).	"They set the priests in their apparel with trumpets, and the Levites the sons of Asaph with cymbals, to praise the Lord, after the ordinance of DAVID king of Israel" (ver. 10).

Moses.	Nehemiah.	David.

Moses.

"They clave to their brethren, their nobles, and entered into a curse, and into an oath, to walk in God's law, which was given by Moses the servant of God" (Neh. x. 29).

David.

"The chief of the Levites ... to praise and to give thanks, according to the commandment of David the man of God" (Neh. xii. 24).

"And both the singers and the porters kept the ward of their God ... according to the commandment of David, and of Solomon his son" (Neh. xii. 45).

This accumulation of evidence furnishes the amplest proof of the Lord's watchful jealousy that Israel should ascribe no ordinances, however great, to His servant Moses besides those which he had given to himself to enact, with an express prohibition against adding more. Yet in these later days men rush in without a shadow of Scriptural warrant, and confiding in their own ingenuity they inform us that they have discovered a whole body of Mosaic laws, which were revealed many hundred years after his death, although they are expressly assigned to Moses by Holy Scripture.

2. The absence of any allusion to the service of song in the sanctuary demonstrates that it was not the design of Deuteronomy, or any section of it, to bring down the institutions of Israel to the time of Manasseh. All advancement in the Deuteronomic code, as compared with the preceding books, had its sufficient cause in the immediate prospect of the occupation of Canaan; but there is not a single law or ordinance in Deuteronomy whose time or occasion of enactment can be shown in the subsequent history. The only isolated enactment in this history is the ordinance of David, that the soldier watching in the camp should share the spoil with those who fought in the battle. The statute is so thoroughly in accordance with the spirit of the laws of warfare in the twentieth chapter of Deuteronomy that it would have formed a most fitting addition to that code. But the honour of Moses was so high in Israel that it was not inserted in what otherwise would have been its appropriate place, but left in its own singularity, as it never would have been if Deuteronomy had been written after its enactment.

But the one great post-Mosaic ordinance in Israel was the ordinance of Praise in the sanctuary; and in the entire book of

Deuteronomy there is not even the slightest allusion to this service, while the whole of the sixteenth chapter consists of special injunctions for the observance of the yearly feasts at "the place which the Lord shall choose." These injunctions are not laid only on men and on families, but on Israel as a nation, including very specially the Levite (ver. 11, 14). "Three times in a year shall all thy males appear before the Lord thy God in the place which he shall choose" (ver. 16). From the days of David downward the service of praise in the sanctuary by cymbal, psaltery, harp, and song, for which four thousand Levites were set apart, formed one of the great characteristics of those annual feasts. But the writer of these laws makes no recognition of such a service. Moses, in Deuteronomy as elsewhere, speaks of God as the object of Israel's praise (chap. x. 21); but no more than in the sacrificial worship of Abraham or Jacob did he appoint any ordinance of song for the service of the sanctuary. If the book were designed as a late supplement to the laws of Moses, this could not by any means have been omitted, for it is the omission of the only great ordinance that is known in history after Moses. The author of Deuteronomy repeatedly enjoins the nation to rejoice before the Lord their God; but so far does he keep from any approach to the national service of cymbal, and harp, and song, that throughout he never calls on Israel even to praise the Lord in the sanctuary. He ordains, "Thou shalt rejoice before the Lord thy God; thou shalt rejoice in thy feast; thou shalt surely rejoice" (ver. 11, 14, 15); and so again in the twelfth chapter (ver. 12): "Ye shall rejoice before the Lord your God, ye, and your sons, and your daughters, and your menservants, and your maidservants, and the Levite that is within your gates." Praise is closely allied to religious joy; yet in the people's thanksgiving for the harvest, which is full of praise, the term itself is not employed. All this tallies most perfectly with the laws and the worship instituted by Moses, and with the service of the tabernacle in his own age and in the ages immediately following. Moses ordained no service of song for the tabernacle, for the song which he taught the people is not given for the priestly or Levitical service at the altar; and he ordained no instrumental praise except that of the two silver trumpets over the sacrifice. Most consonantly, therefore, in commanding Israel to resort to the sanctuary in their holy feasts, he does not call on them to praise the Lord, but earnestly and often exhorts them to "rejoice before the Lord." Such ordinances and injunctions could not have been written in the later days of Israel.

3. But further, the alleged prophetic code in the name of Moses, and with the Divine sanction for its claim of Mosaic authority, would have abolished the service of song in the Temple. That service had no Mosaic sanction, but only the sanction of David, which in legislation was confessedly secondary to the law of Moses. Nothing would have been simpler than, even in a single sentence, to have given the service of praise a Mosaic sanction in Deuteronomy, but no such sanction is given. The melody of the two silver trumpets will still remain, because it was sanctioned by Moses; but a second Moses, with all the authority of the first, supplements the original Mosaic laws, and "brings them down to date," from the days of Moses to the reign of Manasseh, adding all that was needed for this later time, and had been omitted in the earlier laws. If the service of song was deemed worthy of Mosaic sanction, there could be no reason for omitting it in a code which embraces in its minuter precepts matters of much less moment than this great national institution in the worship of God. Yet this second Moses returns to all the severe simplicity of the first, passes by this magnificent worship as if permitted only for a time, and by his silence blots it from the complete code of Mosaic ordinances now presented to Israel. A code under the highest name of Moses, completed down to the days of Manasseh or Josiah, would admit of no institution that was not either formally embraced or in some way sanctioned in its statutes; and this imaginary code of the critics has the glaring inconsistency of cancelling by its silence the glorious ordinance of praise, which has no Divine warrant either under the earlier or the later seal of Moses.

But the beautiful consistency of the Word of God throughout shines all the more brightly through the efforts of its enemies and of its misjudging friends to rend it in pieces. The songs of the sanctuary are denied to David by many critics, who in their lofty misconception alike of God and of man assert it as self-evident, in the nature of things, that the murderer of Uriah could never have been the penitent writer of the 51st Psalm. Yet both the character and the songs of David have in all ages been well understood by broken hearts, because they know that "to whom much is forgiven the same loveth much." So the rationalists have often left to Moses little more than a mythical character, robbing him of most of the Divine words that were given to him as mediating between God and Israel. Still, as in all other respects, so in the light of the ordinance of Praise the words of Moses triumphantly vindicate themselves as his own; as fit for his age and for his lips, but altogether misplaced in the mouth of a prophetic legislator in the time of the later kings of Judah.

CHAPTER VI.

THE JUDICIAL CLEANSING OF THE LAND.

AS Deuteronomy cannot have been designed to bring down the ordinances of Israel to the time of Manasseh because it omits the service of Praise, the only great national institution after the death of Moses; so likewise this cannot have been its design, because it revives the only leading Command of Moses that had become obsolete; or, rather, it originates under his name a command for the destruction of the Canaanites, for if Deuteronomy was not written by him, it cannot be proved that he ever issued such an order.

The stern order in Deuteronomy for ridding the land of Canaan of its ancient races has often been censured as unjust and cruel by the adversaries of the Bible, but in a false sentiment of pity. It was better for the world that Sodom and Gomorrah should be consumed by fire than that they should remain a moral pestilence on the face of the earth. The case was the same with the seven nations of Canaan; who were first warned by the destruction of the cities of the plain, then spared in long-suffering for more than four hundred years after that warning, and finally destroyed only after their iniquity was full by the Divine judgment through the sword of war, as the others had been by the fire of heaven. Their extermination had become an act of mercy to mankind; "For every abomination to the Lord, which he hateth, had they done unto their gods; for even their sons and their daughters had they burned in the fire to their gods" (Deut. xii. 13).

Inconceivably better for the whole world it was that Canaan should be possessed by a nation like Israel than by its former inhabitants; and the stern necessity for their excision was too clearly proved by the corruption of Israel itself through their neglect of the Divine command. On their darkest sin of human sacrifice Ewald writes in his History of Israel:—" The indigenous Canaanite human sacrifice, which was transplanted by the Phœnicians to Carthage, and there kept up to the latest times, was no sign of barbarity common to uncultivated nations, but of the artificial cruelty often arising from excessive polish and over-indulgence. Amid all the changes of time, the moral corruption generated by the seductive charms of such a culture is with difficulty lost in the land of its birth. An effeminacy and depravity of life, not unlike that of the Canaanites, and doubtless promoted in part by the remnant of the early inhabitants, spread to a people which, through their entire nature and laws, ought to have been most proof against it."

The justice and the necessity of the ban of excision in the lips of Moses can be fully vindicated; it was issued in the name of humanity itself, for it lingered long till mercy urged the plea, " Even their sons and their daughters have they burned in the fire to their gods." But in the reign of Manasseh the descendants of the ancient Canaanites had for centuries, from the times of David and Solomon, been under the covenanted protection of the State (1 Chron. xxii. 2; 2 Chron. ii. 17); and the once righteous decree would then have been an order for the perpetration of one of the most treacherous massacres in all history under the name of religion. Except under the influence of strong prejudice, it is impossible to read the book of Deuteronomy without being deeply impressed with the intense desire of the writer that the order should be thoroughly executed by Israel, and his jealousy lest either mistaken kindness, or unbelieving fear, or forgetfulness of the judgment that would fall upon themselves, should hinder its fulfilment. He repeats it in three different sections, and four separate chapters of the book; he allots to it a larger space than to all the Ten Commandments; and he enforces it with all conceivable earnestness.

"When the Lord thy God shall deliver them before thee, thou shalt smite them, and utterly destroy them; thou shalt make no covenant with them, nor show mercy unto them, . . . for they will turn away thy son from following me, that they may serve other gods: so will the anger of the Lord be kindled against you, and destroy thee suddenly. . . . Thou shalt consume all the people which the Lord thy God shall deliver thee; thine eye shall have no pity upon them. . . . Thou shalt not be afraid of them: but shalt well remember what the Lord thy God did unto Pharaoh, and unto all Egypt: . . . thou shalt not be affrighted at them: for the Lord thy God is among you, a mighty God and terrible. . . . He shall deliver their kings unto thine hand, and thou shalt destroy their name from under heaven: there shall no man be able to stand before thee, until thou have destroyed them (chap. vii. 1-24). Understand therefore this day, that the Lord thy God is he which goeth over before thee ; as a consuming fire he shall destroy them, and he shall bring them down before thy face : so shalt thou drive them out, and destroy them quickly, as the Lord hath said unto thee (chap. ix. 3). Of the cities of these people, which the Lord thy God giveth thee for an inheritance, thou shalt save alive nothing that breatheth : but thou shalt utterly destroy them ; . . . that they teach you not to do after all their abominations (chap. xx. 16, 17, 18). And the Lord shall give them up before your face, that ye may do unto them according unto all the commandments which I have commanded you. Be strong and of a good courage, fear not nor be afraid of them " (chap. xxxi. 5, 6).

Professor Davidson represents not his own, but the new theory as coming to not more than this, that the progressive legislation in Israel having been ripened under higher guidance was "thrown back, and represented as the creation of the great mind of the founder of the theocracy; " and he seems to regard this view as at least possible ("Old Test. Exegesis," p. 23). Let the conception be granted for the moment, and let it be borne in mind that the whole foundation of the theory is that the book was written for the age in which it was issued, and for the express purpose of bringing down Mosaic principles to the men of that age in a form adapted to their altered circumstances or more consonant to the gradual development of grace and truth in Divine revelation ; and let it be supposed that decrees and ordinances of such an advanced character are put into the lips of Moses himself. In that case, part of the ordinances may be a repetition of Mosaic laws still in force, like the Ten Commandments ; others will of necessity be new ordinances of importance, else there could be no call for the new legislation ; but that obsolete decrees, the execution of which would in the altered circumstances be in the highest degree criminal, should be introduced into such legislation, for the purpose of " throwing it back," is utterly inconceivable and absolutely monstrous. To mingle modern and practical precepts with archaic commands to Israel to slay the people of the land without mercy, was the likeliest of all means to arouse the nation in an impulse of fanatical zeal, like Saul's against the Gibeonites, to put to the sword the thousands or tens of thousands of the Canaanites, who were now in the land under a covenant of life and safety ; or to embolden an unscrupulous Israelite to entrap some faithful Uriah into a fatal snare, on the ground that the murder of a Hittite proscribed by Divine law was a most worthy deed.

Further, if Deuteronomy was not written by Moses, the author of the book does not faithfully imitate the great lawgiver, but far exceeds him in severity. Except in Deuteronomy, it is doubtful if Moses ever enjoined Israel to put the Canaanites to death with their own hands. He promises that God would partly destroy and partly expel them, and commands Israel to "drive them out" (Exod. xxiii. 31); and many of them, doubtless, abandoned their country before the face of Israel. But there is only a single verse in which he might seem to command Israel to destroy them; our translators take the verse as a command to destroy not them, but their gods; and before Deuteronomy was written this meaning had the preferable claim, as the most lenient interpretation: "Thou shalt not bow down to their gods, nor serve them, nor do after their works: but thou shalt utterly overthrow them, and quite break down their images" (Exod. xxii. 24). But this single and doubtful expression the author of Deuteronomy expands in different places to the extent of a whole chapter, and under every form of the severest denunciation; very naturally in the case of the true Moses, in the hour when Israel was to cross the Jordan, for the purpose of encouraging them in the great war on which they were entering, and of binding on them the severe duties now immediately before them. Now, on such a subject a late imitator of Moses could have had no conceivable motive for going beyond his words; but this supposed author, instead of "throwing back" his own creation into the likeness of the Mosaic precept, carries forward and develops the stern command into a greatly enlarged and strongly enhanced severity.

But the whole idea of these stern decrees against the seven nations of Canaan being fictitious is most uncritical; for, if reality and earnestness can be expressed by human speech, they breathe in every line of these injunctions. It is no mock encounter with the shades of men who had been dead for seven hundred years that is contemplated by the writer; but a terrible conflict with armed men, skilful in war, is to be waged, and no quarter given. This earnestness of the writer for the execution of his commands is so evident and unmistakable that it is fully, although reluctantly, acknowledged by critics most adverse to the Mosaic authorship of the book.

"Had Moses so spoken," writes Kuenen, "with a rough and armed people before him, and the Canaanites in his immediate neighbourhood, it would have been frightful. It now continues to be *seriously meant*, and yet is much more innocent. We are now free to believe, that the sword would have fallen from the hand of the Deuteronomist himself, if it had become necessary to carry out the doom which he had denounced. It is less difficult to murder on paper than in reality."

He owns that a massacre in the days of Josiah was " seriously meant;" and while he calls it " murder on paper," we know that the paper on which was inscribed the order for a massacre of rarely paralleled treachery was never impressed with the seal of the God of truth and mercy.

Professor Oort, of Leyden, is constrained to make the same admission of the earnestness of the writer to put to death the Canaanites who still remained in the land; while his plea in palliation as regards their cities, which applies more specially to chap. xx. 16, does not at all affect the detailed denunciations against the people in the seventh chapter. The extenuation is singular enough, because if there were no such cities remaining, it is a strong argument that these critics have assigned a wrong date to the book. Surely it is extreme presumption in them to assume that their lauded prophet was so devoid of understanding as to issue stringent orders for the destruction of towns which no longer existed. He says:—

" In many respects the writer takes an exalted moral attitude. It is true that he repeatedly urges the Israelites to lay the Canaanites and all other idolaters under the ban; but in this connection it is only fair to remember that when he wrote there were no Canaanite cities in existence, so that in this respect at any rate his injunctions cannot have been intended to be actually put into execution. Nevertheless, we must admit that *he distinctly enjoins a massacre to the glory of God.*"

These exterminating decrees occupy a most leading place in the book of Deuteronomy, in the large amount of space allotted to them, in the various sections of the book in which they are repeated, and in the peculiar earnestness with which they are enforced. If they were embodied in the heart of a book of practical laws only for archaic colouring and poetic thunder, they are the words of " a madman casting firebrands, arrows and death, and saying, Am I not in sport?" But out of all question they were " seriously meant ;" and if of recent date, they are contrary not only to all the laws of God, but to all the traditions of Israel, in their strictest injunctions and strongest incentives to a flagrant breach of covenant by the ruthless massacre of myriads of the peaceful, confiding, and helpless natives of the land. The book, that under the name of law proclaims a ban replete with treachery and death, can form no part of the Word of God, Deuteronomy is blotted out of the Holy Scriptures, our Lord's triple seal to its Divine authority is cancelled, and the whole Bible is lost. Such is the inevitable result of a theory which handles the oracles of God with singular rashness; and entirely perverts one of the plainest books in the Bible, by assigning to it a fanciful origin, and investing it with a fictitious character in direct contradiction to its own express declarations.

CHAPTER VII.

THE ONE ALTAR.

THE evidence most relied on by Dr. Kuenen and others against the antiquity of Deuteronomy is the destruction of the high places by Josiah in obedience to its injunction of a single altar. The high places, however, had been put down by Hezekiah nearly a hundred years before; and if his removal of them was on the same authority as Josiah's, the whole theory falls to the ground. That this was the case is clearly intimated by the inspired authors of the history, for in the reign of Josiah it is said that "Hilkiah the priest found a book of the law of the Lord by the hand of Moses" (2 Chron. xxxiv. 14); and of Hezekiah it is said that "He removed the high places, and brake the images and cut down the groves. . . . He trusted in the Lord God of Israel; so that after him was none like him among all the kings of Judah, nor any that were before him. For he clave to the Lord, . . . and kept his commandments which the Lord commanded Moses" (2 Kings xviii. 4-6). According to the Bible, which is our only source of information, both these kings destroyed the high places in obedience to the law of Moses. Kuenen strenuously holds that Josiah acted according to a written law falsely assigned to Moses; but he asserts that Hezekiah acted by his own authority without any adequate written law :—

"The means which he employed, the 'removing,' 'cutting down,' and 'breaking to pieces,' however suitable they may have been for altering the outward appearance of things in a short time, did not reach the root of the evil. In a word, but little penetration was required to foresee that these violent measures would necessarily be followed by a violent reaction; Amon's death was a blessing for the Mosaic party. . . . Hitherto they had no accurately defined programme. The codes of various ages, which were extant at the beginning of Josiah's reign, had no validity in law. The Mosaic party had to set forth their views plainly and definitely, and to prevail upon the king to carry them out. We have their programme in the book of Deuteronomy."—(*Religion of Israel*, vol. ii., pp. 5, 6, 7, 9.)

The inspired historian who ascribes Hezekiah's conduct to reverence for the law of Moses is thus quite set aside; Dr. Kuenen asserts with the confidence of an eye-witness that his procedure was with the high hand of regal power without any legal warrant; and we are required to confide in this modern discovery as if it were a fact of genuine ancient history. On the basis of so groundless a conception is built the theory of a late Deuteronomy. But such criticism, professing to be rational, is purely arbitrary and unreasonable; and while it claims to be historical, the creative mind of the critic is all the history on which it is founded.

In no light in which it can be regarded does the Deuteronomic ordinance of a single altar indicate an origin for the book in the days of Manasseh or Josiah. The chief elements concerning it in this relation may be embraced in these considerations: The ordinance was not moral but ceremonial, and was not designed to carry its full obligation till after the building of the Temple; the book of Deuteronomy itself enjoins the building of another altar; the law of one altar was never enforced by any penalty, and its neglect is not recorded as entering into Josiah's fears for Jerusalem.

1. The ordinance of one altar was ceremonial, and was to come into full effect only after the building of the Temple. Like other Mosaic institutions, its design was moral; the one altar teaching the unity of God, and well fitted to prepare the minds of Israel for the one great Priest and the one Sacrifice. But the institution was to pass away in the time of the Gospel, and was unknown in the days of the patriarchs. The central altar in Deuteronomy corresponded to the one tabernacle and the one place for the yearly feasts, as enjoined in Exodus. But there is a marked significance in the terms of its institution:—

"When ye go over Jordan, and dwell in *the land* which the Lord your God giveth you to inherit, and when he giveth you *rest* from all your enemies round about, so that ye dwell in safety; then there shall be a place which the Lord your God shall *choose* to cause his name to dwell there; thither shall ye bring all that I command you" (Deut. xii. 10, 11).

The one altar was to be *in the land* of their inheritance when it had become their possession, when they had *rest* from all their enemies, and when the Lord had *chosen* a place for His name to dwell in. In a good measure these three conditions were fulfilled under Joshua before the eastern tribes had returned across the

Jordan: Israel had inherited the promised land, their great war of conquest was finished and followed by rest, and the Lord had set His name in Shiloh. But till the reign of Solomon not one of these conditions had a complete fulfilment; in the days of the Judges Israel had by no means gained possession of all the land, whilst Zion itself was only taken by David; and the fulness of rest was not attained till Solomon could say, "But now the Lord my God hath given me rest on every side, so that there is neither adversary nor evil occurrent" (1 Kings v. 4). It was the same with the third condition of the Lord "choosing a place" for Himself. On this expression great stress is laid in the enactment, and in the twelfth and sixteenth chapters "the place which the Lord shall choose" is repeated eight times over. At the consecration of the Temple (2 Chron. vi.) Solomon says: "The Lord God of Israel spake to my father David, saying, Since the day that I brought forth my people out of the land of Egypt, I chose no city among all the tribes of Israel to build an house in, that my name might be there; but I have chosen Jerusalem, that my name might be there;" in the service of the dedication Jerusalem is five times called the city or the place which the Lord had chosen; and the same designation is used in other Scriptures, but never once except for Jerusalem. The Lord "set His name in Shiloh at the first," but He is not said to have "chosen" it. This distinction is not a verbal one, but real; because while Shiloh had become the place of the Lord's house by the presence of the ark and the tabernacle, there is no record of its peculiar choice by a special recognition, such as twice marked out Zion as selected by the Lord, first by the fire from heaven consecrating Araunah's threshing-floor, and then consuming the sacrifice at the dedication of the Temple, and also by the glory filling all the house. In the inheritance of all the land, in the perfect rest round about, and in the miraculous choice of the place, the conditions of the enactment of a single altar were all at last fulfilled, and the force of the law became complete. From this time forward, no man in the kingdom of Judah who "wholly followed the Lord" offered sacrifice elsewhere than at "the place which the Lord had chosen" in Jerusalem, and in that kingdom God never elsewhere accepted a sacrifice by fire from heaven. One design of this exclusiveness was evidently that after the sacrificial death of Christ Israel should be shut up "without a sacrifice and without an ephod," till "they shall fear the Lord and His goodness in the latter days."

After the division of the kingdom, however, Elijah, the greatest of the prophets next to Moses, offered sacrifice on the altar of twelve unhewn stones which he built on Mount Carmel, and God answered him from heaven. This answer by fire was for the great end of proving to apostate Israel that Jehovah was God, and turning their hearts to Him again; and He had never bound Himself by any ceremonial ordinance. But from Elijah's complaint, "They have thrown down Thine altars," it appears that, during the rending of the kingdom, the godly in Israel had sacrificed on the ancient altars, and that their offerings had been accepted; for the evident reason that they were restrained by force from going up to Jerusalem.

2. In the book of Deuteronomy itself there is an express injunction to build a second altar on Mount Ebal for a great but temporary purpose, an altar of stone in addition to the brazen altar before the tabernacle. The narrative of the erection of the altar by Joshua, in obedience to this commandment, clearly proves that the legislation of Deuteronomy was given by Moses. But, quite apart from Joshua, the altar of Ebal in Deuteronomy disproves the new theory of the origin of the book, according to which one of its chief objects is the absolute injunction of a single altar in the land; for no late prophet, with such an object in view, would have frustrated his own design by inventing a Mosaic command to build another altar besides the central altar before the ark of the covenant. This command issued in the days of Josiah would have been a direct encouragement to Judah even then to build additional altars. Likewise, this altar on Ebal has the important position of proving that the law of the single altar was never designed to set aside such temporary altars as God might expressly sanction. The command, "Take heed to thyself that thou offer not thy burnt-offerings in every place that thou seest," excludes every spot of man's selection, but forbids none that might be designated by God Himself. During the whole time between the death of Eli and the building of the Temple, including the entire judicial life of Samuel, there was no place on which, even in the more restricted sense, it could be said that "the Lord had set His name there," and no altar that could in its full meaning be called "the altar before the Lord." In all that period the ark of the Lord's presence was far apart from the brazen altar and the tabernacle; and it was impossible to obey the enactment so long as this

D

division remained. Other instances of the erection of separate altars by express Divine sanction, as in the case of Gideon and of Manoah, far from being contrary to the book of Deuteronomy, are in most perfect harmony with its injunction of a separate altar on Mount Ebal. In searching the subsequent history for contradictions to the book the critics have overlooked the decisive fact, that the supposed contradiction only brings the history into more exact conformity with the enactments in the book itself. If that history is contrary to the twelfth chapter of Deuteronomy with its one central altar, the twenty-seventh chapter of the book with its altar on Mount Ebal is a still more startling contrariety. This simple fact of the altar on Ebal demonstrates the futility of the whole historic reasons on which the new theory is built, makes it unaccountable how it could ever have been based on such grounds, and brings us back to the position that the law in its very enacting terms was never designed to take its full effect till after the building of the Temple, and was at no time intended to interfere with any altar erected by direct warrant from Heaven. One chief design of the law was to engrave on the heart of Israel the much needed admonition, "Take heed to thyself that thou offer not thy burnt-offerings in every place that thou seest."

3. The law of one altar was enforced neither by penalty under the hand of man nor by threatening of the judgment of God. The connection between the original character of the law and the record of its observance or neglect in the history of Israel, instead of exhibiting an inconsistency, furnishes one of those interesting coincidences between different parts of Scripture which prove their inspiration by one great Author. Every reader of the history of the Kings is struck with the commendation of one after another in the roll of sovereigns who " did that which was right in the sight of the Lord," yet with the qualification, " howbeit, the high places were not taken away; " or more fully, " nevertheless, the people did sacrifice still in the high places, yet unto the Lord their God only." The inspired writers both in Kings and Chronicles stamp this practice with such a character as to indicate that the worshipper did not forfeit the favour or approval of the Most High, although the mode of his worship was marked with censure. The ordinance of a single altar was thus placed on a more elevated level than many other laws, and it was observed only by men who followed the Lord

wholly, like Hezekiah and Josiah, and like eastern Israel returning from Shiloh in the days of Joshua. If the altar erected by these tribes on the western bank of the Jordan had been for sacrifice, their transgression would have been great, although the Temple was not built, because the place was one of their own selection, and the altar was designed as a permanent erection for these entire tribes. But their conscience was tender, the command in Deuteronomy was fresh in their memory, and the very object of their altar was to leave to their children a lasting witness of stone to their inalienable right to sacrifice at the one tabernacle, or in their own words, "to do the service of the Lord before him with their burnt-offerings and sacrifices" (Josh. xxii. 27); so leaving also for us an incontrovertible testimony that the Deuteronomic code was written before Israel had crossed the Jordan.

The historic record of the observance of this law by the nation and its kings, when they were wholly following the Lord, yet not always by men who were pious and sincere, quite accords with the character of the law as regards penalty or threatening. The Mosaic laws were enforced by a penalty under the hand of man, as in the stoning of the nearest relative or closest friend who enticed to the worship of other gods; or by a curse from God through the lips of men, as upon the man who caused the blind to wander out of the way; or by the threatening of Divine judgment, which is understood by the Jews as not requiring the ruler's interference, as against the man who being clean forbore to keep the Passover, and was to be cut off from among his people. But the law of a single altar is one of those ordinances in which there is neither penalty nor curse nor threatening on account of its neglect; there is only the command, with an earnest admonition to take heed to keep it.

This absence of appointed or threatened judgment is in entire harmony with the subsequent history. There were high places to heathen gods, and high places with graven images as in Israel under Jeroboam; the multiplicity of altars tended greatly to increase such heinous offences, and in the most corrupt times there were probably no high places without idols. "They provoked him to anger with their high places, and moved him to jealousy with their graven images" (Ps. lxxviii. 58). But we are not aware that simple altars to Jehovah on high places are ever represented as among the direct causes of the destruction of the nation and desolation of the land; and certainly not either in the prophetic history in Deuteronomy, or the actual history under Josiah. In Deuteronomy when all nations shall ask, "Wherefore hath the Lord done thus unto this land? what meaneth the heat of this great anger? Then men shall say, Because they have forsaken the covenant of the Lord God of their fathers : . . . for they went and served other gods, and worshipped them : . . . and the anger of the Lord was kindled against this land to bring upon it all the curses that are written in this book" (chap. xxix. 24-27). The predicted cause of the judgment is the worship of other gods with all the iniquities it involved. Seven hundred years later, to Josiah trembling for the words of the Book, and inquiring at the prophetess Huldah, the answer is exactly the same : "Tell ye the man that sent you to me, thus saith the Lord, Behold, I will bring evil upon this place, and upon the inhabitants thereof, even all the curses that are written in the book which they have read before the king of Judah : because they have forsaken me, and have burned incense unto other gods, that they might provoke me to anger with all the works of their hands; therefore my wrath shall be poured out upon this place, and shall not be quenched" (2 Chron. xxxiv. 23-25). In the words of the prophetess, exactly as in Deuteronomy, there is no reference whatever to the neglect of the law of a single altar as the cause, or as one of the causes, of the Lord's anger, but only to the worship of other gods.

In this whole subject of the ordinance of a single altar, there is not the slightest contradiction, but the most entire harmony, between the original law of Moses and the subsequent history of Israel. But the command to erect an altar on Mount Ebal, if first issued in the reign of Josiah, is a most direct contradiction of the alleged leading design of the second Moses regarding a single altar at Jerusalem.

CHAPTER VIII.

THE LAW OF THE FIRSTLINGS.

IF the objection to Deuteronomy as truly Mosaic on the ground of its ordinance of a single altar in Israel had any reasonable foundation, no fault could be found with it as of slight importance. But this cannot be said of a crowd of small objections on the regulation of sacrifices and other matters, in which it is alleged that Deuteronomy directly contradicts the Levitical legislation; the wonder rather being that so diligent a search finds no greater difficulties to be removed in a book of statutes so ancient, and so many of them relating to observances with which we are not practically conversant. At these minute differences we need not stumble, even if we cannot now explain them. Yet in some of the confidently alleged instances, the difficulty is not to reconcile the contradiction, but to discern it; as when Moses in the wilderness absolutely enjoins the offering of every firstling fit for sacrifice, and afterwards on the eve of Israel's entrance into Canaan relaxes or alters the command, if the owner should be living at a distance from the sanctuary. In other cases it is to be remembered that some statutes will of necessity seem obscure if they are not read with care.

Instead of entering into a number of little details, let us select out of these alleged contradictions the instance that seems to have been oftenest adduced and pressed: the acknowledged gift in Numbers xviii. 15-18 of the firstlings to the priests, and the alleged assignation of them to every Israelite in Deut. xii. 17, 18; xiv. 23; xv. 19, 20. Without disparaging the solutions that have been offered, we submit these considerations as amply sufficient to remove any apparent difference, taking as our guide the statute in the twelfth chapter as serving to explain the others that follow.

1. The Deuteronomic code can never be clear except we bear

in mind as a leading rule in its interpretation, that Moses is addressing the *nation* as well as its individual men, and that he often speaks to the community as if to one man :—

"Out of heaven he made thee to hear his voice, that he might instruct thee. . . . To drive out nations from before thee greater and mightier than thou art. . . . Thou shalt therefore keep his statutes, . . . that it may go well with thee, and with thy children after thee (chap. iv. 36, 38, 40). Three times in a year shall all thy males appear before the Lord thy God. . . . And thou shalt rejoice before the Lord thy God, thou, and thy son, and thy daughter, and thy man-servant, and thy maid-servant, and the Levite that is within thy gates, and the stranger, and the fatherless, and the widow, that are among you, in the place which the Lord thy God hath chosen to place his name there (chap. xvi. 10, 11). Thou shalt separate three cities for them in the midst of thy land (chap. xix. 2). Judges and officers shalt thou make thee in all thy gates. . . . Thou shalt not wrest judgment ; thou shalt not respect persons, neither take a gift" (chap. xvi. 18, 19).

Besides personal precepts, such as to help a brother whose ox had fallen down in the way, there are many of these national commands in the singular number, yet passing as if into personal injunctions for children, for son and daughter. The expression, "within thy gates" does not mean that each Israelite had cities of his own ; nor was each one to appoint cities of refuge or judges, or to execute justice without bribery ; but these things were to be done in the community. So in chapter xii. 17, "Thou mayest not eat *within thy gates* the tithe of thy corn, or of thy wine, or of thy oil, or the firstlings of thy herds or of thy flock : . . . but thou must eat them before the Lord thy God in the place which the Lord thy God shall choose," is a command to the nation and not to the individual, and defines nothing on the personal duties of different classes of the community.

2. The statutes in the chapter in which the command first occurs, and also the subsequent passages, are written with a very special reference to the place which the Lord should "choose" in the promised land. It is evidently the special object of the whole chapter not to define the *persons* who are to offer the sacrifices or to eat of the offerings, but the *place* where they are to be offered and to be eaten. The persons had been exactly defined in Numbers xviii., and now the place is specified as the one sanctuary in the land which the Lord would choose. This is so marked as the object of the chapter (xii. 1-28), that the expression "the place which the Lord shall choose" is repeated five several times (vers. 5, 11, 14, 18, 26), and five times more in the expressions "thither"

shall ye bring them, and "there" shall ye eat. In the eighteenth of Numbers there is nothing said about "the place which the Lord shall choose," but only about the priests ministering at the tabernacle; and there are very precise rules laid down regarding the participation in holy things by the priests and their sons, or by all in their house both sons and daughters. In Deuteronomy there is nothing of this kind, but there are equally strict injunctions about the place where the offerings are to be presented and to be eaten. It is therefore most reasonable to interpret the first set of laws as defining the persons, and the second as defining the place without specifying the persons; and to accept the command, "Thou shalt eat" as addressed to Israel, and to be interpreted in accordance with the previous statutes.

3. This interpretation of the law of firstlings is not only in itself reasonable and probable, but as explained by the context must be held to be absolutely certain. The critics who refuse these laws to Moses cannot reconcile the eighteenth verse of the eighteenth of Numbers, giving the firstlings to the priests, and the eighteenth verse of the twelfth of Deuteronomy, giving them as they conceive to every Israelite; but they omit all notice of the much more startling contradiction in these chapters between the seventh verse in Numbers and the twenty-seventh in Deuteronomy, which completely disproves their interpretation of these laws. In Numbers the priest alone is to offer sacrifice on the altar, and it is death for any other, either Israelite or Levite, to intrude into this office; but according to this new reading of the law in Deuteronomy every Israelite is to be his own priest, and positively commanded to offer his own sacrifice on the altar:—

"Thou shalt offer *thy burnt-offerings, the flesh and the blood, upon the altar* of the Lord thy God: and the blood of thy sacrifices shall be poured out upon the altar of the Lord thy God, and thou shalt eat the flesh" (Deut. xii. 27).

The first law forbids, under pain of death, the Israelite to do that which the second law expressly commands him to do; yet our opponents are far from holding that every Israelite was constituted a priest. But "thou shalt eat," in the eighteenth verse, and "thou shalt offer," in the twenty-seventh, are undoubtedly addressed to the same persons; and if the offering must be understood not of every Israelite, but of Israel through those already appointed for that privilege, so must also the eating. The contradiction is not in the laws themselves, but in the evidently mistaken interpretation now put upon them.

4. The same passage also cancels the favourite objection of the want of distinction in Deuteronomy between the priests and the Levites, which is thus stated by Professor Davidson:—

"In the Levitical books there is a sharp distinction between priests and Levites. ... In Deuteronomy mention is made of priests and Levites, but the state of things is this :—Levi is the priestly tribe, all Levites may be priests, but of course all are not, and the distinction between priests and Levites is, that priests are actually officiating Levites. ... Let any one consider the sharp distinction drawn in the middle books with the tragic histories connected with it, and then say whether it is probable that a few years after no allusion to the distinction should appear in the course of a whole book" (p. 18).

We are not aware of any foundation for the statement that all Levites may be priests; for evidently Deuteronomy xviii. 6-8 only proves that the Levite who quitted his home for the sake of the sanctuary should be welcomed to take part in its ministrations with his brethren already there; and the frequent expression, "the priests the Levites," simply designates the priests as sons of Levi, and intimates that all the priests were Levites, but certainly not that a priest was merely an officiating Levite. Nowhere is the distinction between priests and Levites more strongly marked than in the account of Hezekiah's reformation in the 2nd Book of Chronicles—" He brought in the priests and the Levites . . . and said unto them, Hear me, ye Levites. . . . And the priests went into the inner part of the house, . . . and brought out all the uncleanness that they found in the temple of the Lord. . . . And the Levites took it, to carry it out abroad into the brook Kidron. . . . And he commanded the priests the sons of Aaron to offer on the altar of the Lord" (xxix. 4, 5, 16, 21). There are many similar expressions of the distinction. Yet the closing account of the Passover is in these words: "Then the priests the Levites arose and blessed the people" (chap. xxx. 27); proving that after denoting the priests as the sons of Aaron, and repeatedly making an express distinction between them and the Levites, the inspired writer could quite naturally and consistently call them "the priests the Levites." Dr. Davidson's argument, founded on its not being "probable" that the sharp distinction between priests and Levites drawn by Moses in the Levitical books would be quite omitted in Deuteronomy if he had written it, is a fair illustration of the foundation on which a great mass of innovating criticism rests; not only because the actual is so often different from the probable, but also because what is probable to one mind may be quite the reverse to another. To his mind the facts that Moses had previously made the lines of distinction so plain, and that the consequences of denying them had been so tragic, make it not probable that in his last address to Israel he should have omitted to repeat or enforce the distinction; although it must be remembered that he does not omit to recall to their memory the awful judgment on those who abetted the deniers of the Divine distinction (chap. xi. 6). To our mind, again, nothing seems more probable than that Moses should have regarded the clear and definite statutes he had already given on the high office of the priesthood, and their terrible vindication, as ample reasons for not repeating them. Who is to decide between us with our contrary probabilities? and is our probable or improbable any ground whatever for originating or defending these most perilous innovations on the holy oracles of God?

But the command in Deuteronomy xii. 27 settles this whole section of the controversy, and proves that this entire line of argument rests on a misconception of the character of the book. Clearly it does not belong to the design of the book to define again the distinctions between the different classes of the community which had been sufficiently marked already; and it omits these distinctions with an implied reference to the Levitical books in which they had been exactly laid down. On any other supposition this statute would be fatally misleading, for it might be understood as conferring the priesthood on the whole people; and according to the new interpretation this must be the meaning of the command. We look in vain through the book for any authority given to the Levite to assume the priestly office; but, interpreted by this view of its legislation, the statute not only allows, but enjoins every Israelite, each Ephraimite, and Benjamite to officiate as his own priest, and lay his own burnt-offering on the altar. The interpretation is, therefore, absolutely wrong; and the object of these enactments is evidently to lay these duties and confer these priviliges on the *nation* of Israel, to be discharged or enjoyed by the different classes in the State, in accordance with the distinctions already laid down in the Levitical ordinances.

5. Returning to the law of firstlings, the contradictory interpretation, so far as we know, is a recent one, and most certainly

it is not the ancient reading of these laws. Nehemiah was well acquainted with the law of Moses; and he had practical as well as traditional helps for knowing it, such as we do not now possess. The book of Deuteronomy was in his memory, or in the memory of those with whom he united in prayer, and its testimony is cited for Israel, that " their feet had not swelled nor their raiment waxed old for forty years in the wilderness " (Deut. viii. 4; Neh. ix. 21). It was also in his hands, and he refers to its written command concerning the Ammonite and the Moabite, not by the unknown prophet of modern discovery, but "in the book of Moses " (Deut. xxiii. 3; Neh. xiii. 1). But he had never discerned any change in Deuteronomy regarding the firstlings; for if he had, he would certainly have followed it. Accordingly, he does not give the firstlings to all the people, but expressly assigns them to the priests; and he assigns them to the priests according to the law of Moses :—

"They entered into an oath, to walk in God's law, which was given by Moses the servant of God, and to observe and do all the commandments of the Lord our Lord, . . . and to bring the first-fruits of our ground, . . . also the first-born of our sons and of our cattle, *as it is written in the law,* and the firstlings of our herds and of our flocks, to bring to the house of our God, *unto the priests that minister in the house of our God* " (Neh. x. 29, 35, 36).

He obeys the law of Moses in Numbers by giving them to the priests, and he obeys the law of Moses in Deuteronomy by giving them to be eaten " in the place which the Lord had chosen to put His name there." The contradiction is not in the law of God, but in the imaginary discoveries of men.

CHAPTER IX.

THE TESTIMONY OF JOSHUA.

THE Book of Joshua is commonly and justly believed to have been written by Joshua himself, or else by one of "the elders that overlived him," who as comrades in his march could speak of the waters of the Jordan being dried up " until we were passed over" (chap. v. 11). For our present purpose, however, it is enough that it was undoubtedly written before the marriage of Solomon, for it speaks of the Canaanites dwelling in Gezer "unto this day" (chap. xvi. 10), which must have been previous to Pharaoh's capture and gift of that city as a portion to his daughter (1 Kings ix. 16); and it must for a similar reason have been written before David took the fort of Zion from the Jebusites (2 Sam. v. 6, 7), whom it describes as dwelling in Jerusalem "unto this day" (chap. xv. 63). If, then, the book of Joshua was not written by himself, or by one of his elders, as we believe it to have been, its date is at least earlier by several centuries than the new date assigned to Deuteronomy.

But there is the amplest evidence that Joshua was written, not before, but after Deuteronomy, as an express sequel to its legislation, and a record of the historical fulfilment of its commands and its promises. It seems impossible to read the one book after the other without accepting this conclusion as at once natural on the surface of their contents, and undeniable under a closer inspection; and it appears unaccountable to assign a recent date to Deuteronomy without making Joshua still later, and agreeing with those critics who hold that it was written either by the same author, or by another in the later days of Judah. As an imperfect substitute for the consecutive reading of the books themselves, let us select out of each some of the corresponding passages that are peculiar to these two books:—

I. DEUTERONOMY.

"Every place whereon the soles of your feet shall tread shall be yours: from the wilderness and Lebanon, from the river, the river Euphrates, even unto the uttermost sea shall your coast be" (chap. xi. 24).

"There shall no man be able to stand before you (chap. xi. 25). Be strong and of a good courage: for thou must go with this people unto the land which the Lord hath sworn unto their fathers to give them; and thou shalt cause them to inherit it. The Lord . . . will be with thee; he will not fail thee, neither forsake thee (chap. xxxi. 7, 8). Thou shalt not go aside from any of the words which I command thee, to the right hand, or to the left (chap. xxviii. 14). He shall read therein all the days of his life; . . . that he turn not aside from the commandment, to the right hand, or to the left" (chap. xvii. 19, 20).

"I commanded you at that time, saying, The Lord your God hath given you this land to possess it: ye shall pass over armed before your brethren the children of Israel, all that are meet for the war. But your wives, and your little ones, and your cattle, . . . shall abide in your cities which I have given you; until the Lord have given rest unto your brethren, as well as unto you, and until they also possess the land which the Lord your God hath given them beyond Jordan: and then shall ye return every man unto his possession, which I have given you" (chap. iii. 18, 19, 20).

JOSHUA.

"Now after the death of Moses, . . . the Lord spake unto Joshua, saying, . . . Every place that the sole of your foot shall tread upon, that have I given unto you, *as I said unto Moses*. From the wilderness and this Lebanon even unto the great river, the river Euphrates, all the land of the Hittites, and unto the great sea toward the going down of the sun, shall be your coast."

"There shall not any man be able to stand before thee all the days of thy life: as I was with Moses, so I will be with thee: I will not fail thee, nor forsake thee. Be strong and of a good courage: for thou shalt cause this people to inherit the land (*marg.*) which I sware unto their fathers to give them. . . . According to all the law, which Moses my servant commanded thee: turn not from it to the right hand or to the left. . . . This book of the law, . . . thou shalt meditate therein day and night" (chap. i. 1-8).

"Remember the word which *Moses the servant of the Lord commanded you*, saying, The Lord your God hath given you rest, and hath given you this land. Your wives, your little ones, and your cattle, shall remain in the land which Moses gave you on this side Jordan; but ye shall pass before your brethren armed, all the mighty men of valour, and help them; until the Lord hath given your brethren rest, as he hath given you, and they also have possessed the land which the Lord your God giveth them: then ye shall return unto the land of your possession, and enjoy it, which Moses the Lord's servant gave you on this side Jordan" (chap. i. 13, 14, 15).

The entire tenor of these opening verses of the book of Joshua agrees exactly with the book of Deuteronomy. The commands to Joshua to "be strong and of a good courage," and not to turn from the commandment "to the right hand or to the left;" and the promises that "the Lord will be with him," and "neither fail nor forsake him," that "no man shall be able to stand before him," and that he shall "cause the people to inherit the land," are all peculiar to Deuteronomy; and the repetition of the words of Moses out of that book is with the obvious design of making the history a sequel to the legislation. Not only so, but in Joshua the grand initial promise to Israel of the gift of "every place whereon the sole of their foot shall tread," is expressly stated to be according to the saying of the Lord to Moses; and it is only in Deuteronomy that we find this promise so graphic in its terms, and in this respect so distinct from all the other promises to the nation. This one citation determines the relative dates of the two books; for the author of Joshua begins his book with the statement that the Lord had spoken these words to Moses, and therefore Deuteronomy must have been written before Joshua. In like manner, Joshua takes his address to the two tribes and a-half nearly word for word from Deuteronomy, and he begins it with ascribing the words to the great lawgiver of Israel, "Remember the word which Moses the servant of the Lord commanded you."

II. DEUTERONOMY.

"Of the cities of these people, which the Lord thy God doth give thee for an inheritance, thou shalt save nothing alive that breatheth; but shalt utterly destroy them" (chap. xx. 16, 17).

"If a man have committed a sin worthy of death, . . . and thou hang him on a tree: his body shall not remain all night upon the tree, but thou shalt in any wise bury him that day: (for he that is hanged is accursed of God;) that thy land be not defiled, which the Lord thy God giveth thee for an inheritance" (chap. xxi. 22, 23).

JOSHUA.

"He utterly destroyed all that breathed, as the Lord God of Israel commanded (chap. x. 40). Neither left they any to breathe. As the Lord commanded Moses, . . . so did Joshua; he left nothing undone of all that the Lord commanded Moses" (chap. xi. 14, 15).

"The king of Ai he hanged on a tree until eventide: and as soon as the sun was down, Joshua commanded that they should take his carcase down from the tree (chap. viii. 29). He slew them, and hanged them on five trees: . . . And . . . at the time of the going down of the sun, Joshua commanded, and they took them down off the trees" (chap. x. 26, 27).

DEUTERONOMY.	JOSHUA.
"Caleb the son of Jephunneh; ... to him will I give the land that he hath trodden upon, and to his children, because he hath wholly followed the Lord" (chap. i. 36).	"Moses sware, ... Surely the land whereon thy feet have trodden shall be thine inheritance, and thy children's for ever, because thou hast wholly followed the Lord thy God" (chap. xiv. 9).
"There shall no man be able to stand before you: for the Lord your God shall lay the fear of you and the dread of you upon all the land that ye shall tread upon" (chap. xi. 25).	"And the Lord gave unto Israel all the land which he sware ... unto their fathers; and there stood not a man of all their enemies before them" (chap. xxi. 43, 44).

Except in Deuteronomy, it is doubtful if the people were ever expressly commanded with their own hands to destroy the Canaanites; and it is certain that in it alone, and in its central code, the command is given in the words to "save alive nothing that breathed," which are repeated in these exact terms as fulfilled by Joshua.

The curse on him "that hangeth on a tree," so well known to us through its transformation into a blessing by the death of the Son of God in our stead, we find written only in Deuteronomy, which is full of sayings treasured by our Lord and His apostles, and precious to the Church in all ages. As the accompanying command that "his body shall not remain all night upon the tree" is peculiar to the central legislation of Deuteronomy, so its execution is recorded nowhere in the Old Testament except in the book of Joshua, in which there is thrice narrated a careful removal of the dead bodies at the setting of the sun, and certainly as part of the great record that "Joshua left nothing undone of all that the Lord commanded Moses."

The narrative in Joshua of Caleb "claiming the land whereon his feet had trodden," of no man having been "able to stand before" Israel, as afterwards of their dwelling in "cities which they built not," and "eating of vineyards and oliveyards which they planted not," is in the words of Deuteronomy; and the account is given for the purpose of proving how completely and exactly all the promises by Moses had now been fulfilled to Israel.

III. DEUTERONOMY.

DEUTERONOMY.	JOSHUA.
"On the day when ye shall pass over Jordan unto the land which the Lord thy God giveth thee, thou shalt set thee up great stones and plaister them	"Then Joshua built an altar unto the Lord God of Israel in mount Ebal; as Moses the servant of the Lord commanded the children of Israel, as it is

DEUTERONOMY.	JOSHUA.
with plaister, ... in mount Ebal.... And there shalt thou build an altar unto the Lord thy God, an altar of whole stones: thou shalt not lift up any iron tool upon them.... And thou shalt offer burnt-offerings thereon:... and thou shalt offer peace-offerings.... And thou shalt write upon the stones all the words of this law very plainly" (chap. xxvii. 2-8).	written in the book of the law of Moses, an altar of whole stones, over which no man hath lift up any iron: and they offered thereon burnt-offerings unto the Lord, and sacrificed peace-offerings. And he wrote there upon the stones a copy of the law of Moses, which he wrote in the presence of the children of Israel" (chap. viii. 30-32).

In the record of this great transaction, the writer of the book of Joshua has the injunction in Deuteronomy before him; he repeats its exact words, and expressly assigns it to Moses as its author. At the same time he gives what one cannot but receive as a clear and unequivocal testimony to the fact that the Deuteronomic legislation was written by the great lawgiver himself, with the national assembly for his witnesses. "He [Joshua] wrote there upon the stones [not of the altar, for it had just been said that on it no iron was to be lifted, but on the stones spoken of in Deuteronomy] a copy of the law of Moses, which he [Moses] wrote in the presence of the children of Israel."

The account of the erection of the altar in Mount Ebal by Joshua, according to the command of Moses, is so clear and full as it now stands in the Bible, that its seal to the Mosaic authorship of Deuteronomy can scarcely be said to be controverted, for the argument against it that appears to be confided in is the plea of interpolation. From the earliest ages of Christianity this plea has been resorted to in defence of views rejected by the Church, and it can only be regarded as a confession of weakness, unless very special reasons can be adduced for the perilous expedient; but no such reasons are given by Bleek, in his Introduction to the Old Testament, on this passage in Joshua:—

"There is here a clear and even literal reference to Deut. xxvii., where all this had been ordained by Moses; and if we compare the two, we cannot doubt that they were written down by *one* author, both the ordinance by Moses and the execution by Joshua, in the way it here runs. This section of the book of Joshua (chap. viii. 30-35) shows itself pretty clearly to be a later interpolation in the rest of the history, as the passage following (chap. ix. 1), 'When all the kings . . . ,' cannot from its purport relate to the section immediately preceding, but only to the capture of Ai, as is indeed clearly shown in v. 3. The section, therefore, appears to have been inserted here by the author of Deuteronomy." *

* Similarly, Professor Smith, Additional Answer, p. 87: "The passage about the altar on Mount Ebal appears to be a late interpolation after Deuteronomy."

This would be a grave imputation against the fidelity of the supposed author, only it is light after the Deuteronomic fiction has been imputed to him. But without even an alleged plea of difference in the Hebrew manuscripts, mere abruptness in the narrative is an incredibly slight ground for such a supposition, because of necessity the account of this religious transaction must have occupied a parenthetic place in the history of the conquest of the land. The altar of unhewn stones was to be erected by Israel in Mount Ebal at the earliest opportunity after the crossing of the Jordan, and their secured possession of the part of the country in which it stood; and as the transaction itself, so the Scriptural account of it intervenes in the midst of the progressive military occupation of the country. It is their abruptness and brevity that help to give their inimitable charm and unfailing interest to the Biblical narratives, alike in the Old Testament and the New, and enable the writers to record in a natural and vivid narrative many great and instructive events in the compass of a few chapters.

IV. Deuteronomy.	Joshua.
"If ye shall diligently keep all these commandments which I command you, to do them, to love the Lord your God, to walk in all his ways, and to cleave unto him (chap. xi. 22). To walk in all His ways, and to love him, and to serve the Lord thy God with all thy heart and with all thy soul" (chap. x. 12).	"Take diligent heed to do the commandment and the law, which Moses the servant of the Lord charged you, to love the Lord your God, and to walk in all his ways, and to keep his commandments, and to cleave unto him, and to serve him with all your heart and with all your soul" (chap. xxii. 5).

These commands in Joshua are both quoted from Deuteronomy, and expressly stated to have been charged on Israel by Moses, thus giving the most direct testimony both to the antiquity of Deuteronomy and to Moses as its author. If it be argued that some parts of the passage may be gathered from the other books of Moses, the remark will apply only to individual expressions, and not to the command as a whole, while other expressions, such as "walking in all his ways," are only found in Deuteronomy. Specially the expression "to cleave," which is frequently used to denote close adhesion, as of the clods of earth cleaving fast together, or of the tongue cleaving to the roof of the mouth, is rare as applied to the Lord; and we are not sure if it is elsewhere found in this sense, except in the utterance of David's attachment to his God, "My soul cleaveth after Thee" (Ps. lxiii. 8), and in the beautiful type of Jeremiah's girdle. It occurs twice in Joshua (xxii. 5; xxiii. 8), and five times in Deuteronomy (iv. 4; x. 20; xi. 22; xiii. 4; xxx. 20), and never in the other laws of Moses. But Joshua here tells the children of Israel explicitly that Moses charged them to "*cleave* unto the Lord," and gives thus a very distinctive testimony to the laws of Deuteronomy as the word of Moses himself.

V. DEUTERONOMY.

"Take heed to thyself that thou offer not thy burnt-offerings in every place that thou seest: but in the place which the Lord shall choose in one of thy tribes, there thou shalt offer thy burnt-offerings, and there thou shalt do all that I command thee" (chap. xii. 13, 14).

JOSHUA.

"God forbid that we should rebel against the Lord, and turn this day from following the Lord, to build an altar for burnt-offerings, for meat-offerings, or for sacrifices, beside the altar of the Lord our God that is before his tabernacle" (chap. xxii. 29).

The cordial agreement of the twelve tribes of Israel, brought out in the striking narrative of the altar Ed, that they would neither build nor tolerate any rival to the brazen altar before the tabernacle, presents a remarkable indication of the deep impression made on the whole nation by the fervent address of Moses on the banks of the Jordan: and if Josiah's jealousy for the central altar is rightly taken by the critics as a proof that he had found the book of Deuteronomy, the much more notable jealousy of the entire nation for the same ordinance would be maintained by them as a still more remarkable proof of their possession of that book, except for a misleading prejudice.

VI. DEUTERONOMY.

"Take heed to yourselves, that . . . ye turn not aside, and serve other gods, and worship them; and then the Lord's wrath be kindled against you; . . . and ye perish quickly from off the good land which the Lord giveth you" (chap. xi. 16, 17).

"When the Lord thy God shall have brought thee into the land which he sware unto thy fathers, . . . to give

JOSHUA.

"When ye have transgressed the covenant of the Lord your God, which he commanded you, and have gone and served other gods, and bowed yourselves to them; then shall the anger of the Lord be kindled against you, and ye shall perish quickly from off the good land which he hath given unto you" (chap. xxiii. 16).

"I have given you a land for which ye did not labour, and cities which ye built not, and ye dwell in them; of

DEUTERONOMY.	JOSHUA.
thee great and goodly cities, which thou buildedst not; . . . vineyards and olive-trees, which thou plantedst not" (chap. vi. 10, 11).	the vineyards and oliveyards which ye planted not do ye eat" (chap. xxiv. 13).
	"There failed not ought of any good thing which the Lord had spoken unto the house of Israel; all came to pass" (chap. xxi. 45).

These passages from the closing chapters of Joshua are all taken in substance from Deuteronomy, and in part they are quoted from it word for word. They prove that, as in the first chapter and onwards, so likewise to the end of the book, the author of Joshua had the words of Deuteronomy in his hands or in his memory. It is specially and expressly from the words of Deuteronomy that he brings out the great conclusion which his book was written to prove, that "there failed not ought of any good thing which the Lord had spoken unto the house of Israel; all came to pass."

The comparison we have thus made of passages from these two books proves that the author of the book of Joshua had the book of Deuteronomy before him, and wrote with a design of showing the correspondence of the history with the words of Moses as there recorded. This designed agreement involves these conclusions:—

(1.) If Joshua is an authentic history, Moses was the author of Deuteronomy.

(2.) If Deuteronomy was a legislative fiction written under one of the later kings of Judah, the history of Joshua is not authentic; but one of its designs was to throw a cloud of apparent historic truth over that fiction by a narrative embodying a fictitious fulfilment of its words.

(3.) If the book of Joshua is a fiction, even the delusive plea of literary form, as of parable or drama, cannot be offered on its behalf; it is either a genuine history of the conquest of Canaan, or falsehood of an aggravated character.

(4.) Therefore the opinion, that Deuteronomy or its legislation was written seven hundred years after Moses, involves the conclusion that the book of Joshua is not inspired; and to believe, nevertheless, that it is inspired can have no effect in altering this conclusion, which is necessarily involved in assigning Deuteronomy to this late period.

CHAPTER X.

THE SEAL OF THE NEW TESTAMENT.

1. THE frequent appeals by our Lord and His apostles to the words of Deuteronomy as Divine are so many seals to its authenticity as the writing of Moses; because it is only by the greatest violence that its source as from God can be severed from its communication to us by the hand of Moses, and if its strictly Mosaic origin is denied its Divine inspiration can never be defended. That the Jews in the time of our Lord held it as an essential part of the law of Moses is allowed by all; and as such it is transmitted to us with the seal of the New Testament, everywhere without the slightest intimation that a large portion of the law had no connection whatever with Moses: "The law came by Moses: we have found him of whom Moses in the law and the prophets did write: they have Moses and the prophets, let them hear them: did not Moses give you the law: beginning at Moses and all the prophets, he expounded the things concerning himself: *first*, Moses saith, I will provoke you to jealousy by them that are no people (Deut. xxxii.); but (afterwards) Esaias is very bold, and saith, I was found of them that sought me not." In the law given by Moses, Deuteronomy was included by the Jews and by the writers of the New Testament, quite as much as Exodus; and the later of the two books would no more have been assigned by them to another author than the earlier.

2. Our Lord's testimony to Moses as the author and the writer of the book of Deuteronomy, in answer to the inquiry of the Pharisees on the lawfulness of divorce, is clear and explicit (Mark x. 2; Deut. xxiv. 1). He asks what Moses commanded; and when they appeal to Deuteronomy for his sanction, He sets that sanction aside, but not at all on the ground that the book was not really the writing of Moses, which would to them have been the strongest of all arguments. On the contrary, He expressly declares "he

(Moses) wrote you this precept," assigning not only the giving of the law but the writing of it to Moses; and explaining the inward motive of Moses in granting the sufferance, "For the hardness of your heart he wrote you this precept." This must mean Moses in his own person, and not an ideal representation of him; nor is it God, who is spoken of on the contrary as ordaining the original institution; but the man Moses under the Divine guidance. Such a testimony ought to have been revered as a Divine arrest on the new theory, and to have debarred it from spreading beyond the bounds of rationalism.

3. The martyr Stephen, full of the Holy Spirit, in replying to the charge of saying that "Jesus of Nazareth shall change the customs which Moses delivered," first refers to Moses bringing Israel out of Egypt; then says, "This is that Moses which said unto the children of Israel, A Prophet shall the Lord your God raise up unto you of your brethren, like unto me, him shall ye hear" (Acts vii. 37); and then expressly declares that this prediction in Deuteronomy was uttered by him who led Israel out of Egypt. The Apostle Peter, in laying the foundation of the Christian Church, cites the same great prediction as the utterance of Moses: "For Moses truly said unto the fathers, A Prophet shall the Lord your God raise up unto you of your brethren, like unto me;" and the force of his argument with the Jews depends on the truth of the prophecy as coming from Moses himself. He is speaking to them in the name of One who claimed to be greater than Moses, and the apostle reasons with them on the ground that Moses had testified that such a Prophet was to be raised up in Israel, like to himself; like him in speaking with God face to face, in mediating between God and the people, and in giving laws to Israel with Divine authority. His argument is that Moses himself is a witness for Christ; and to his hearers it would have been very different indeed had they been told that an unknown Prophet, seven hundred years after the death of their great lawgiver, had foretold that Moses would be superseded by Jesus of Nazareth.

But to us as well as to Israel the historical foundation of the New Testament as engrafted on the Old is undermined by the new theory of the date and origin of this great prophecy. If it is not the true but an ideal Moses that utters the words "A Prophet like unto me," then Moses himself at Mount Sinai ceases to be a living man, and becomes merely an idea; not that the bare existence of the man Moses is set aside, but that the whole transactions at Mount Sinai, and all similarly marvellous events either are, or may be purely ideal. The words of Moses on the plains of Moab, "The Lord thy God will raise up unto thee a Prophet like unto me" (Deut. xviii. 15), are his dying assurance to Israel on the express ground of what God had said to himself on Mount Sinai, "I will raise them up a Prophet like unto thee," in consequence of the people's desire not to hear again the voice of God Himself (ver. 16-18). According to the new theory, this promise on Mount Sinai of the great future Prophet is purely ideal, and was given seven hundred years afterwards. Now, Deuteronomy, as the latest revelation invested with Mosaic authority, supersedes Exodus in so far as it differs from it; and as the latest Mosaic revelation, it must likewise be our authoritative guide in the interpretation of the previous records. But if the Lord's answer to Moses in the 17th and 18th verses, that the people have well spoken in asking a mediator with God, and that he will raise up for them another prophet, is not a true but an ideal answer, never given to Moses at all, then the people's request in the 16th verse must likewise be ideal, for their petition and the Divine reply are parts of one transaction. The people's prayer without the answer is recorded also in Exodus (chap. xx. 19); but if, according to the latest authoritative document, this request of the people on Mount Sinai is ideal and not actual, it must be lawful, if not incumbent, to interpret the whole scene in Exodus ideally; and to follow the most destructive critics in holding that not even the Ten Commandments, as we now have them, are really in the words of Moses. If the Deuteronomist was not Moses, he is a Prophet greater than Moses; but such a Prophet was impossible, except in the person of the Messiah.

Professor Davidson, without directly noticing the prediction of the great Prophet, takes up the concluding verses of the passage and reasons against their authenticity by an argument that is alarmingly bold in dealing with the Holy Scriptures:—

"The prophecy in Deuteronomy regarding the prophets seems directed to meet the ramifications and developments of a pseudo-prophecy—sometimes consciously false, and sometimes, perhaps, self-deceived—such as history makes us familiar with. But this pseudo-prophecy arose only side by side with true prophecy, and came to a head during the moral confusions and political perplexities of the time before and after Jeremiah. We cannot help asking whether a statement from

Moses about prophecy was *likely* to take into account and frame itself so as to meet such a peculiar condition of the national mind, the result of such distant and complicated historical movements? And this is just an instance of the kind of questions which meet us everywhere in this field " (p. 17).

The prophecy of Moses regarding the Great Prophet is a signal prediction of a very distant event; but his directions how to distinguish between true prophets and false are so fitted to meet a not unlikely evil, as scarcely to come under the class of unlikely predictions. But if our acceptance of prophecy is to be squared by what its interpreters deem "likely;" and if on account of the prediction of circumstances, "the result of distant and complicated historical movements," a prophecy is to be rejected as unlikely; the truth of many of the greatest prophecies in the Bible is destroyed. Let us return to the words of holy writ in the mouth of the first of the apostles: " Moses truly said unto the fathers, A Prophet shall the Lord your God raise up unto you like unto me;" and in the lips of our Lord Himself: "Had ye believed Moses, ye would have believed me, for he wrote of me; but if ye believe not his writings, how shall ye believe my words?"

All of us agree in believing in Deuteronomy as an undoubted portion of the inspired Scriptures, both because it was received and honoured as such by the Hebrew nation, and because we have the ample testimony of our Lord and His apostles to its Divine authority. But some have hastily supposed that if, on the ground of such a sanction, they cordially accept it as inspired, the historical truth of its outward form is of little moment. When, however, the historical truth is once abandoned, there is no ground left on which to defend the Divine authority; and however individual men, retaining their loyalty to their Lord, may hold fast the truth after they have undermined its foundation, it is to be feared that the greater number will follow out consistently the path on which they have been persuaded to enter, will go on to reject the historical and prophetical truth first of the Old Testament and then of the New, and will either roam in a dreary path that has no solid ground beneath it, or fall into the dark abyss of a hopeless unbelief.

The Word of the Lord is pure, and out of this trial it will come forth in all its brightness as silver out of the furnace. But, meanwhile, an unutterable calamity may overtake us, for our children may lose the one treasure we were bound to bequeath to them; and for long years they may wander "through dry places seeking rest, and finding none," before they recover their hold of the Word of Life, and regain their footing on the rock of eternal truth.

The following words of warning have come to us only too seasonably from another land :—" From the scene of His temptation and conflict, in His ordinary teaching, when surrounded and pressed by the cavilling Jews, from the risen Lord, and just as the opening heavens were to receive Him from our sight, we have one, repeated, unvarying, consistent testimony of Christ that Moses was the author of the Law.

"It does not meet the case at all to say that Christ accommodated Himself to the prevalent view of His day, that He was only using popular language, adapting Himself to the prejudices of His hearers; for that involves one of two things which lie in the face of the whole Gospel, or involves both. Either that Christ was a mere man, and shared in the prejudices and ignorance of His age; or Christ lent His great name and authority to sanction and perpetuate common errors, and errors which touched the spiritual interests and life of the people. Those who agree fully with KUENEN and COLENSO may say that Christ was ignorant as those around Him, or at least shared in that ignorance; and it must be confessed that this is a less abysmal depth than the supposition of moral obliquity. In either case, however, the Christ of the Gospels has disappeared.

"We are shut up to this alternative. Either we must abide by the testimony of Christ, and regard Moses as the author of Deuteronomy, or we may accept the premisses and conclusions of these negative critics, and thus part with our Bibles and Christ." *

---

* Lange's Commentary on the Old Testament. DEUTERONOMY, by Rev. F. W. J. Schröeder; with Appendix by the Rev. Dr. Gosman, from which we have taken this extract, p. 272. We had not seen the volume till after the preceding pages had been printed.

www.ingramcontent.com/pod-product-compliance
Lightning Source LLC
Chambersburg PA
CBHW020731100426
42735CB00038B/1871